Excel Essentials

A Step-by-Step Guide with Pictures
for Absolute Beginners to Master
the Basics and Start Using
Excel with Confidence

NIGEL TILLERY

EXCEL ESSENTIALS 2023

EXCEL ESSENTIALS 2023

TABLE OF CONTENTS

Chapter 1: Introduction..9

1.1 The Value of Excel Training 9

1.2 A Summary of the Contents of the Book....................9

1.3 Using the Excel User Interface.....................10

Chapter 2: Making and Saving Workbooks......................16

2.1 Starting a Fresh Workbook.............................16

2.2. Save Your Work....................................18

2.3 Simple File Administration.........................24

Chapter 3: Working with Cells, Rows, and Columns 31

3.1 Addressing and Cell References................................31

3.2 Choosing Rows, Columns, and Cells.........................31

3.3 Adding and Removing Columns and Rows.............37

3.4 Modifying Column Width and Row Height 40

3.5 Cells that Merge and Unmerge..................................41

Chapter 4: Entering and Formatting Data 44

4.1 Text and Number Entry 44

4.2 Formatting Cells 46

4.3 Applying Number Formats..............................49

4.4 Making Use of Border and Fill Colors 51

Chapter 5: Basic Formulas and Functions 54

5.1 Developing Basic Formulas 54

5.2 Using Foundational Features.........................56

5.3 Understanding Relative and Absolute Cell References 62

5.4 Formulas for Copying and Pasting 66

Chapter 6: Sorting and Filtering Data 68

6.1 Data Sorting by One or More Columns 68

6.2 Using Filters to Show Particular Data 71

6.3 Eliminating Duplications................................75

Chapter 7: Data Visualization with Charts and Graphs 79

7.1 Type of Graphs 79

7.2 Chart Design 82

7.3 Making Your Chart Your Own 85

7.4 Modifying and Editing Data for Charts 90

EXCEL ESSENTIALS 2023

Chapter 8: Tips and Preparing Your Spreadsheet for Printing **96**

8.1 Making the Print Area 96

8.2 Altering Page Size and Orientation...........................98

8.3 Addition of Headers and Footers 103

8.4 Checking Your Spreadsheet Out and Printing It 104

Chapter 9: Advice for Excel Newcomers **107**

9.1 Keyboard shortcuts 107

9.2 Actions You Can Undo and Repeat........................ 108

9.3 Utilizing the Help Function 110

9.4 Organizational Best Practices for Spreadsheets..... 112

Chapter 10: Conclusion and Next **114**

Chapter 11: Bonus **119**

A Special Invitation to My Readers

Hi and welcome to "Excel Essentials 2023"!

I'm Nigel Tillery, and I'm delighted that you've chosen this book as your guide to mastering Excel. As you dive into the upcoming chapters, you'll find essential tools and techniques that I've laid out to help you get started on your Excel journey.

But I don't want our conversation to end when you turn the last page. To further enrich your experience and learning, I'd like to invite you to join my **Excel Excellence Newsletter**.

In this newsletter, I'll be sharing:

- **Advanced Excel features** that can make your life easier
- **Time-efficient** methods that I personally use to make the most out of Excel
- **Expert advice** for tackling some of Excel's more complex problems

I created the newsletter to be a valuable resource for you—one that complements this book and helps you grow your skills even further.

So, if you're interested in extending your Excel education, simply copy the following link or scan the QR code.

https://jo.my/excelessentialsnewsletter

Together, we'll make sure you're fully equipped to excel in Excel.

Warm regards,

Nigel Tillery

Chapter 1: Introduction

1.1 The Value of Excel Training

Powerful spreadsheet software like Microsoft Excel has become a necessity for professionals in a variety of fields. Learning Excel may make it easier for you to organize and analyze data, create budgets, keep track of sales, and quickly complete complicated computations. Employers place a high value on Excel skills, which may lead to new work prospects and professional progress

1.2 A Summary of the Contents of the Book

This Excel Beginner's Guide to learning spreadsheets aims to provide new Excel users with a strong foundation. The following subjects will be covered in the book:

- Developing and preserving workbooks
- Utilizing rows, columns, and cells
- Data entry and formatting
- Basic functions and formulae
- Data filtering and sorting
- Visualizing data with graphs and charts
- Creating pages for printing
- Advice for Excel newcomers

When you finish reading this book, you'll fully grasp Excel's fundamentals and be prepared to use it productively.

1.3 Using the Excel User Interface

While working on your spreadsheets, you will interact with various parts of the Excel interface. You can use the program to its fullest extent and navigate it more effectively if you are familiar with these components.

1.3.1 The Ribbon

The main toolbar in Excel is the Ribbon, located at the top of the window. It is divided into tabs, such as Home, Insert, Page Layout, and Formulas, each of which has a collection of tools and instructions that are relevant to that tab. When a tab is clicked, the tools and settings it corresponds to are displayed.

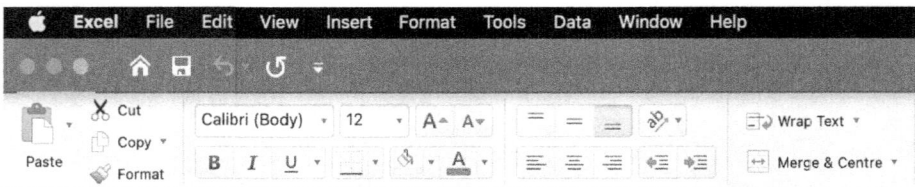

1.3.2 Quick Access Toolbar

The top-left area of the window's Quick Access Toolbar offers quick access to frequently used actions, including Save, Undo, and Redo. You may add or remove commands from the Quick Access Toolbar to fit your tastes.

EXCEL ESSENTIALS 2023

1.3.3 Formula Bar

The active cell's contents are shown in the Formula Bar underneath the Ribbon. When a formula or function is entered into a cell, it is shown in the Formula Bar and may be edited there.

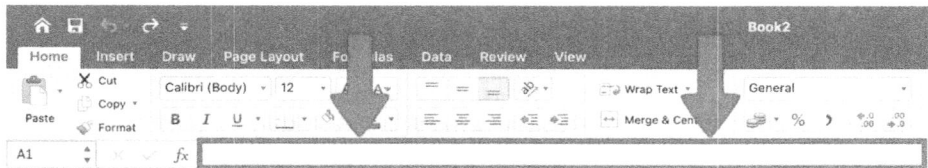

1.3.4 Worksheet Area

The Worksheet Area consists of a grid of cells arranged in rows and columns and is Excel's primary workspace. Each cell has a specific address (for example, A1, B2, C3) based on its row and column positions. You may use these cells to insert and modify data as you build your spreadsheets.

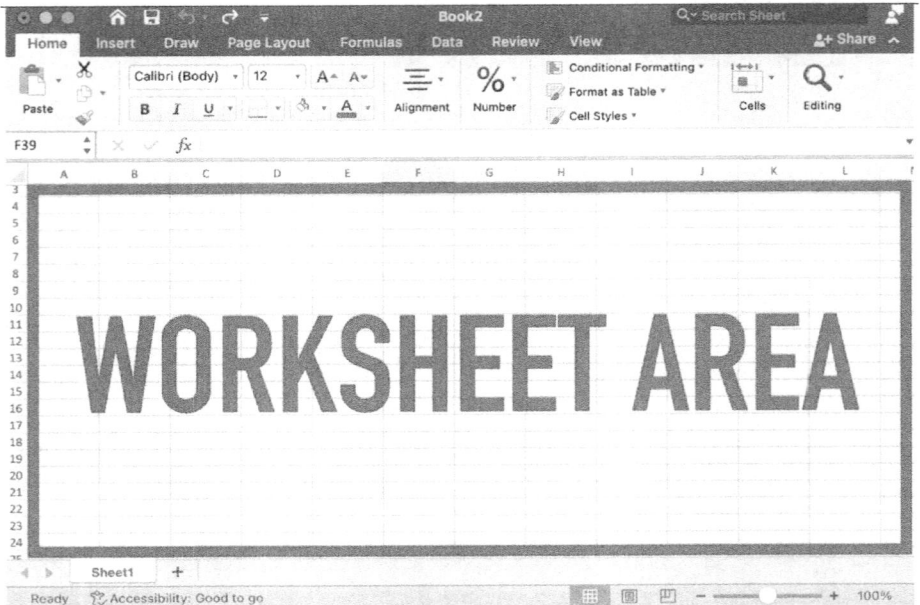

1.3.5 Sheet Tabs

Sheet Tabs, which allow you to switch between worksheets inside a workbook, are located at the bottom of the window. A new workbook comes with one worksheet by default, but you may add additional ones as necessary.

EXCEL ESSENTIALS 2023

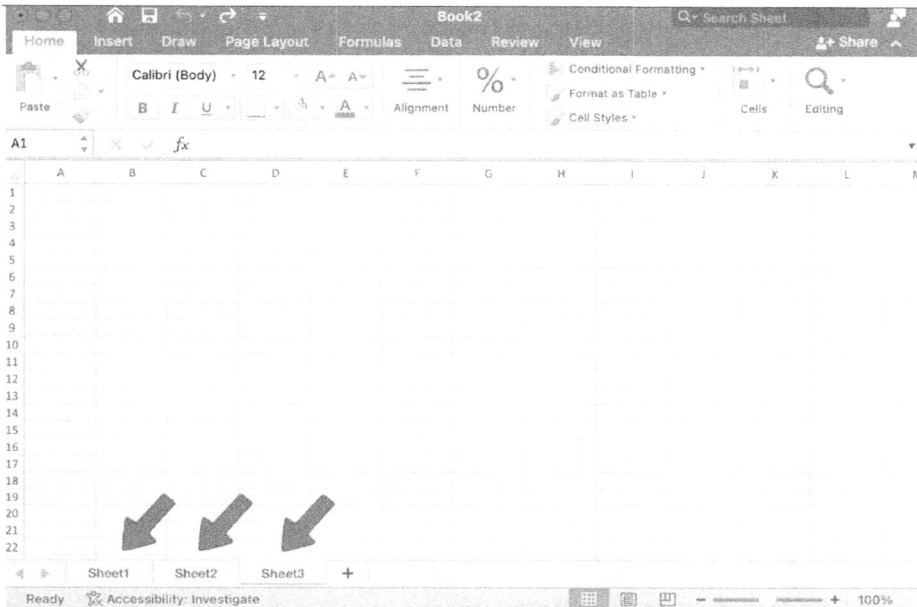

1.3.6 Status Bar

The status bar, visible at the bottom of the window, details the condition of the workbook, such as the number of selected cells, and calculation results for specific data, such as total or average.

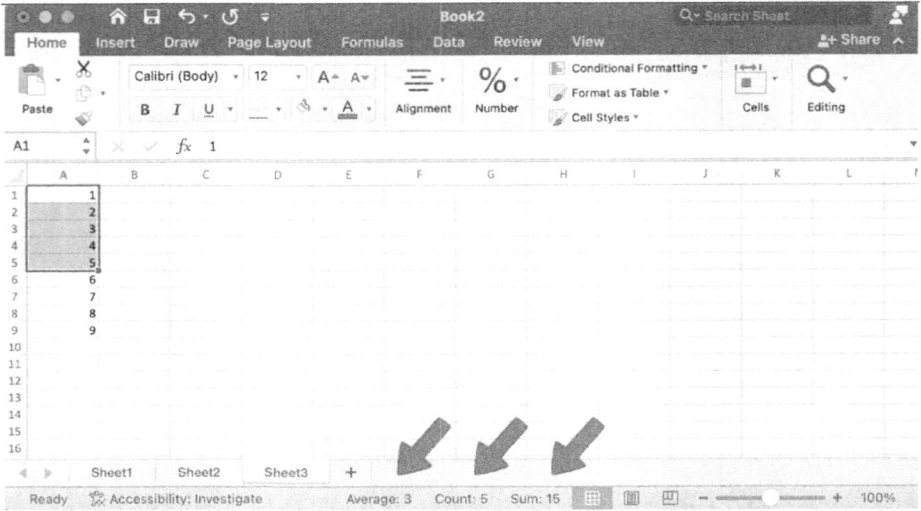

1.3.7 Zoom Adjustments

The Zoom Controls, located in the bottom-right corner of the window, allows you to change the worksheet's level of magnification. To examine and manipulate your data more quickly, you can zoom in and out using the slider or the plus and minus buttons.

EXCEL ESSENTIALS 2023

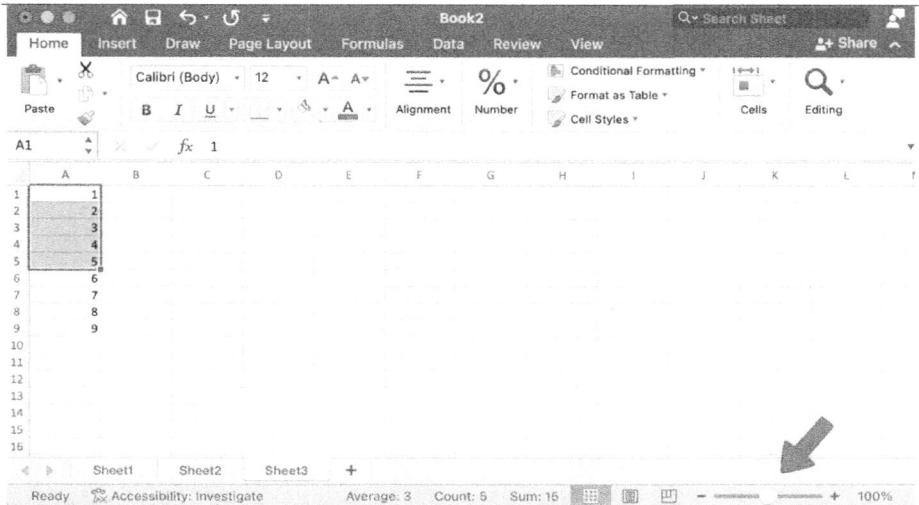

You are now prepared to start making and using spreadsheets since you have a fundamental grasp of Excel. The following chapters will walk you through Excel's basic features and capabilities to help you become an expert user of this potent program.

Chapter 2: Making and Saving Workbooks

2.1 Starting a Fresh Workbook

You must open a new worksheet in Excel before you can begin working. We refer to an Excel file containing one or more worksheets as a workbook.

Get Microsoft Excel going.

You can immediately go to work if the workbook is empty when the program launches. If not, choose "New" from the "File" option on the Ribbon.

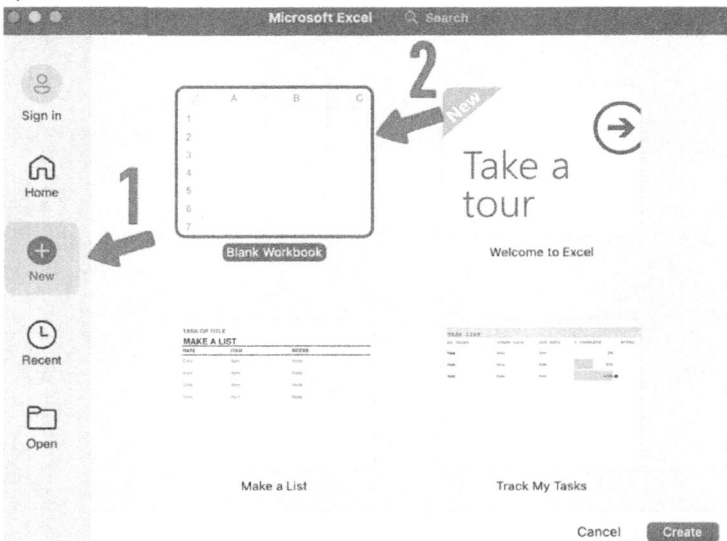

Or from the list of templates, select "Blank Workbook".

EXCEL ESSENTIALS 2023

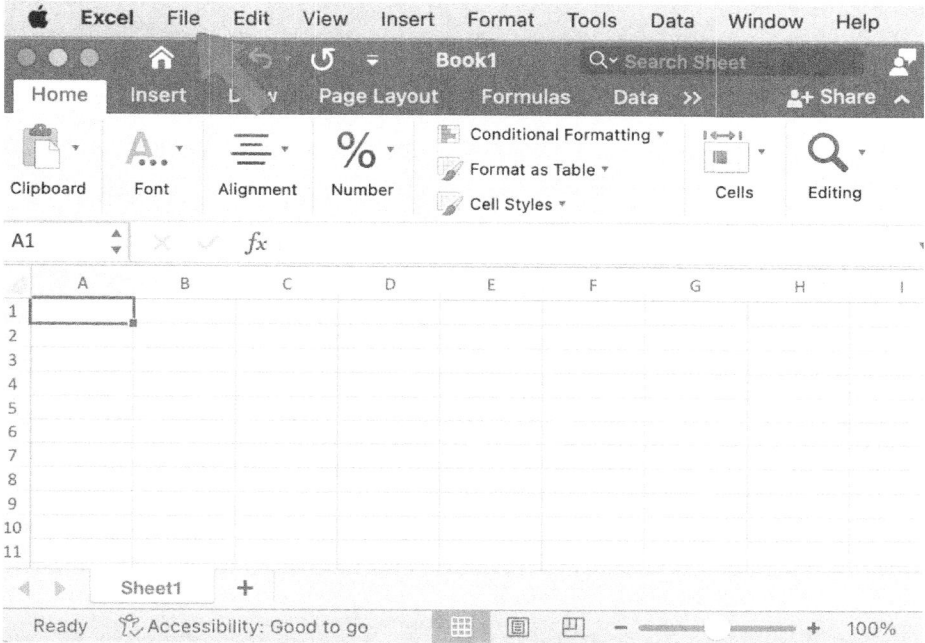

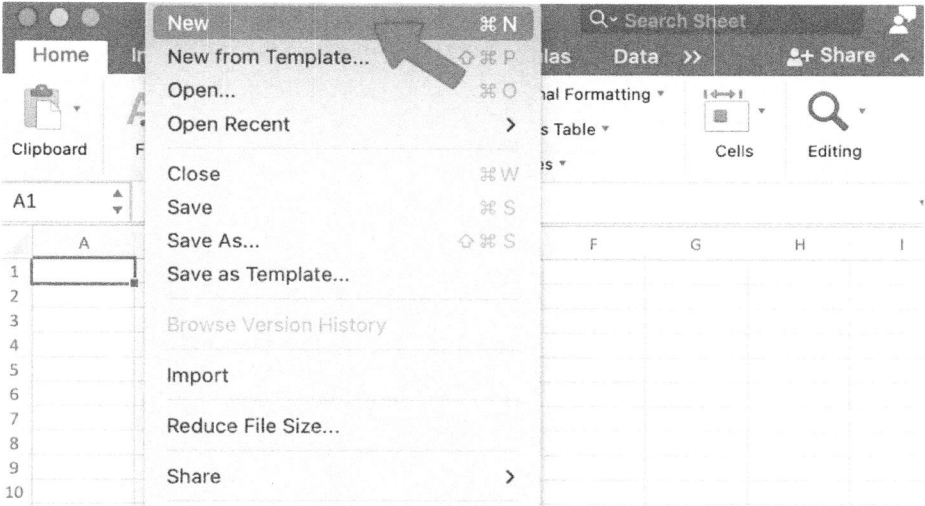

Now that the new workbook is blank, you may start entering data and making spreadsheets.

2.2. Save Your Work

To avoid losing any information or progress, it's important to save your work routinely. Excel offers numerous options for saving workbooks:

2.2.1 First-Time Workbook Saving

Follow these procedures to save a workbook for the first time:
In the Ribbon, choose the "File" tab and select "Save."

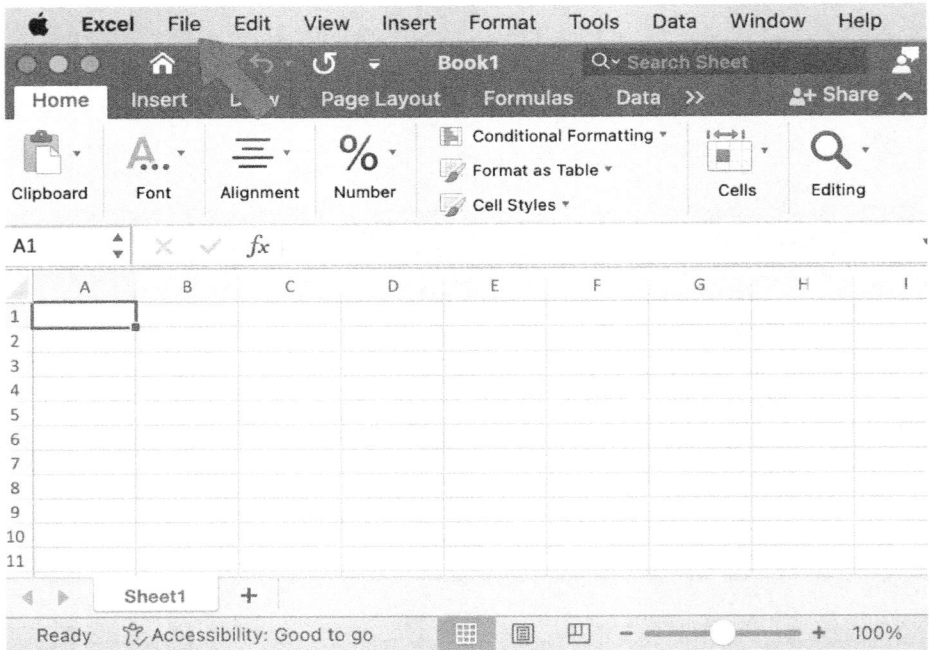

EXCEL ESSENTIALS 2023

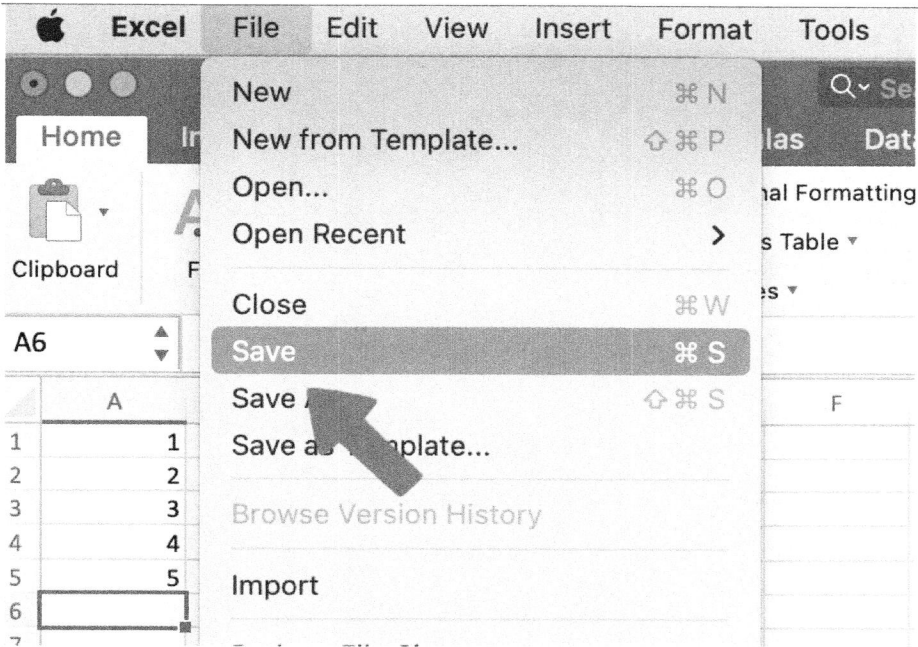

Wherever you wish to save your file, select that place.

In the "File name" box, type an explicit file name.

Set the "Save as type" dropdown menu to "Excel Workbook (*.xlsx)."

Select "Save" from the menu.

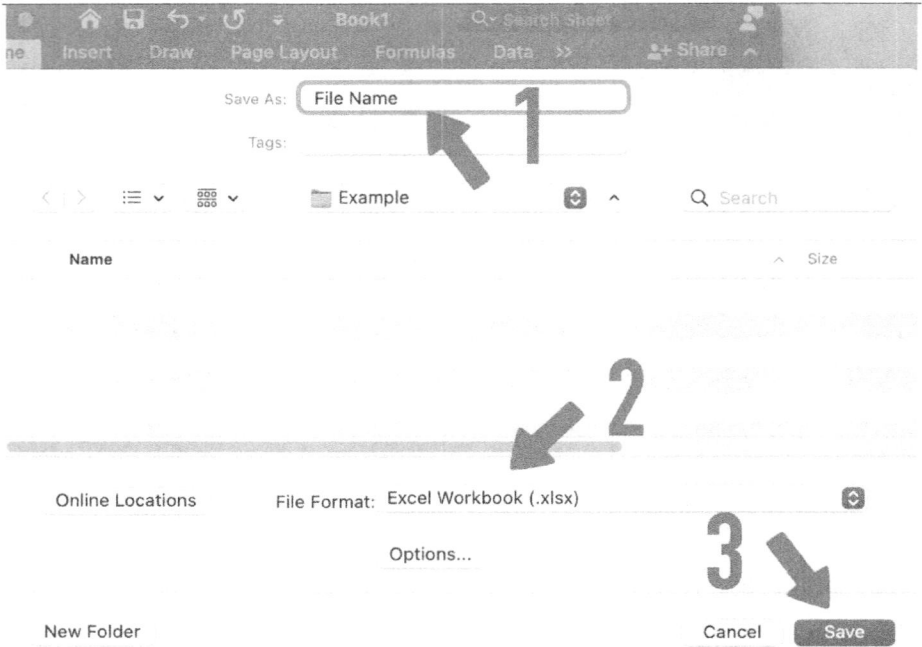

You have now saved your workbook in the desired file and folder.

2.2.2 Save Modifications to an Existing Workbook

It's essential to save your changes often while you work with Excel. To save changes to a workbook that already exists, you may use one of the following techniques:

You can find the "Save" button (the floppy disk icon) in the Quick Access Toolbar.

EXCEL ESSENTIALS 2023

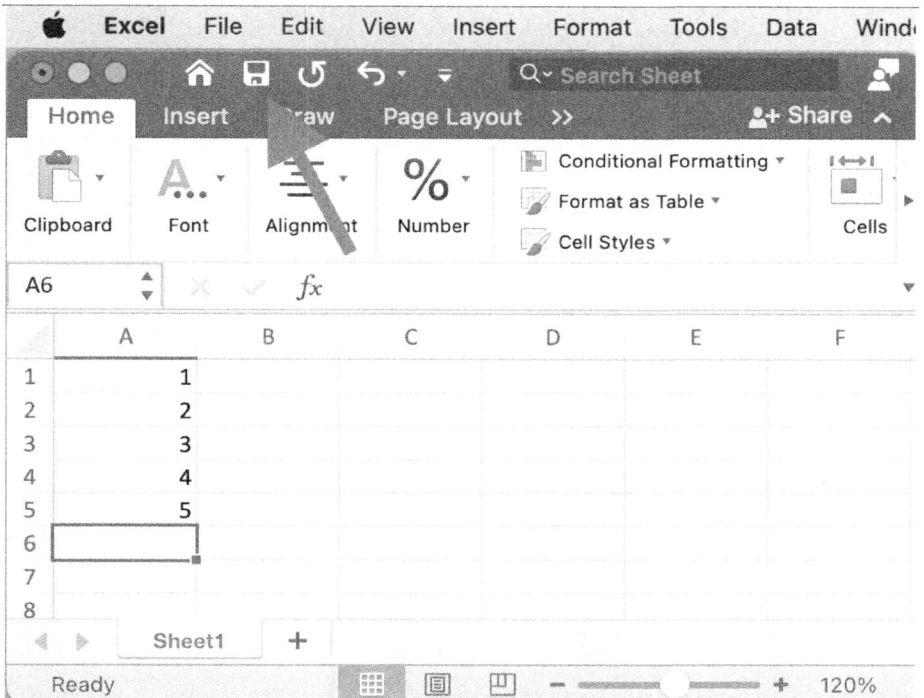

Hit "Ctrl + S" on your keyboard.

Choose "Save" from the "File" tab on the Ribbon.

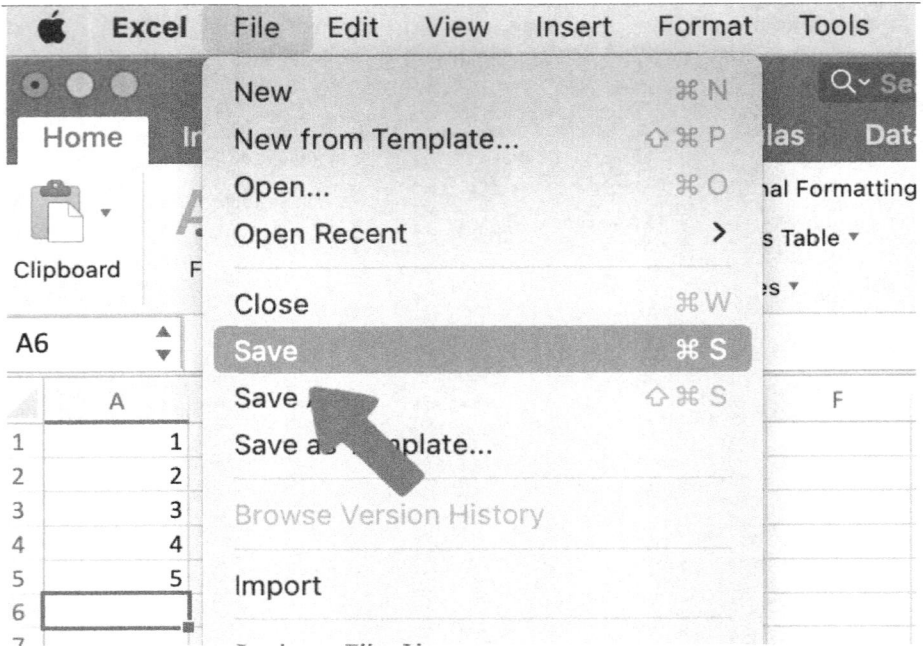

2.2.3 Store a Workbook Copy

You can use the procedures below to create a duplicate of your workbook with a different file name or location:

In the Ribbon, choose the "File" tab and select "Save As."

EXCEL ESSENTIALS 2023

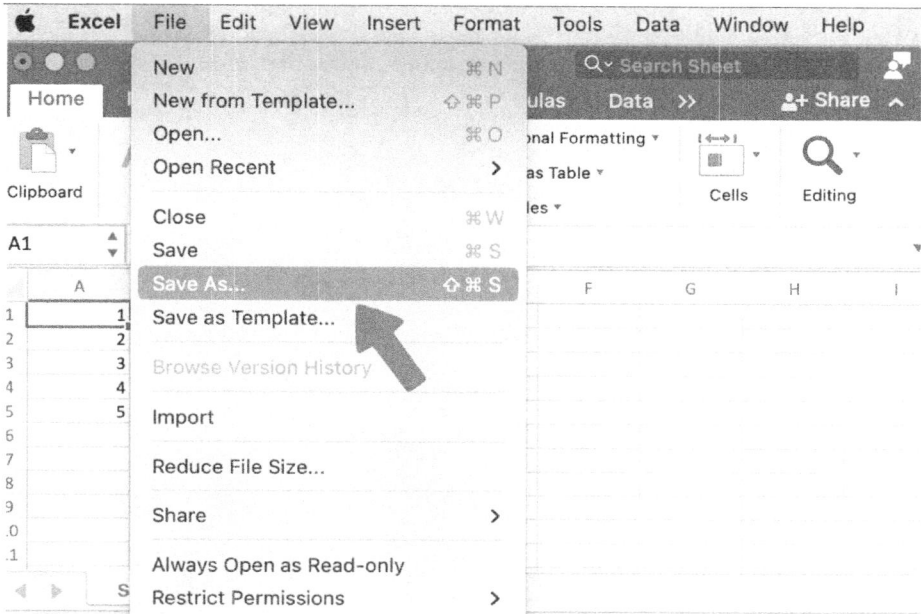

You may select the place to store the duplicate.

In the "File name" box, type a new file name.

Set the "Save as type" dropdown menu to "Excel Workbook (*.xlsx)."

Select "Save" from the menu.

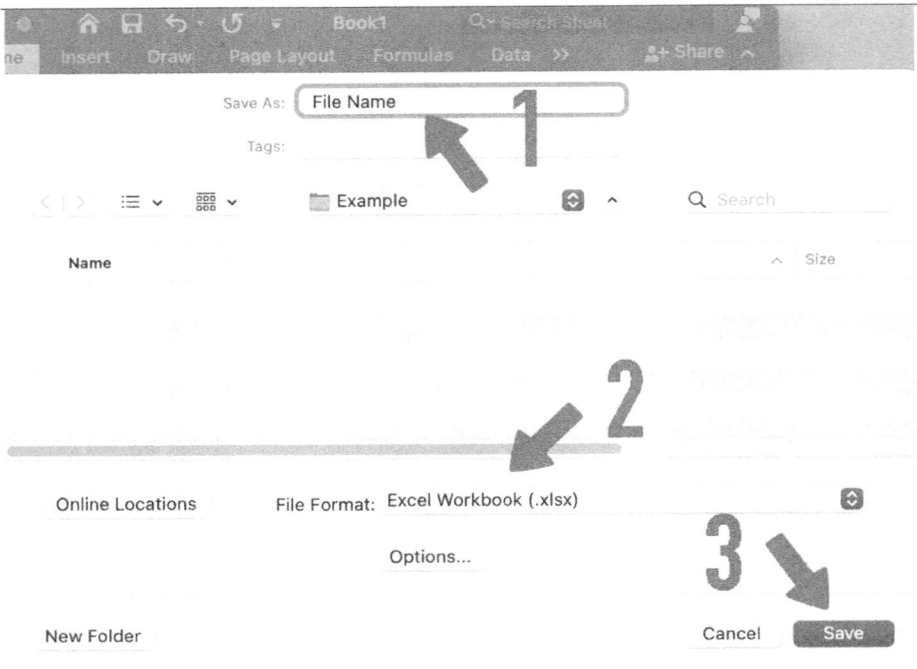

You have now saved your workbook with the updated file name and location.

2.3 Simple File Administration

You can stay organized and easily retrieve your work by managing your Excel files properly. While using Excel, you may need to carry out the following important file management tasks:

2.3.1 Accessing a Previous Workbook

Follow these procedures to open an existing workbook:

EXCEL ESSENTIALS 2023

Click the "File" tab in the Ribbon and choose "Open."

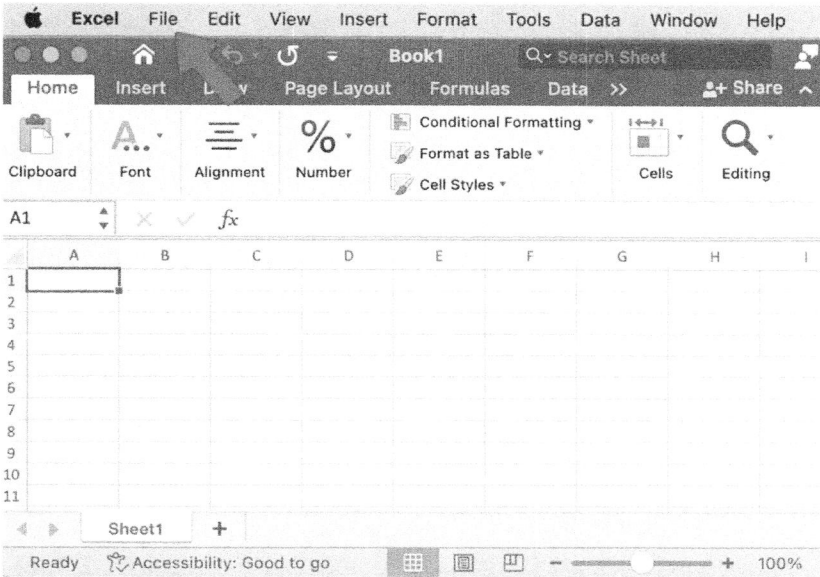

EXCEL ESSENTIALS 2023

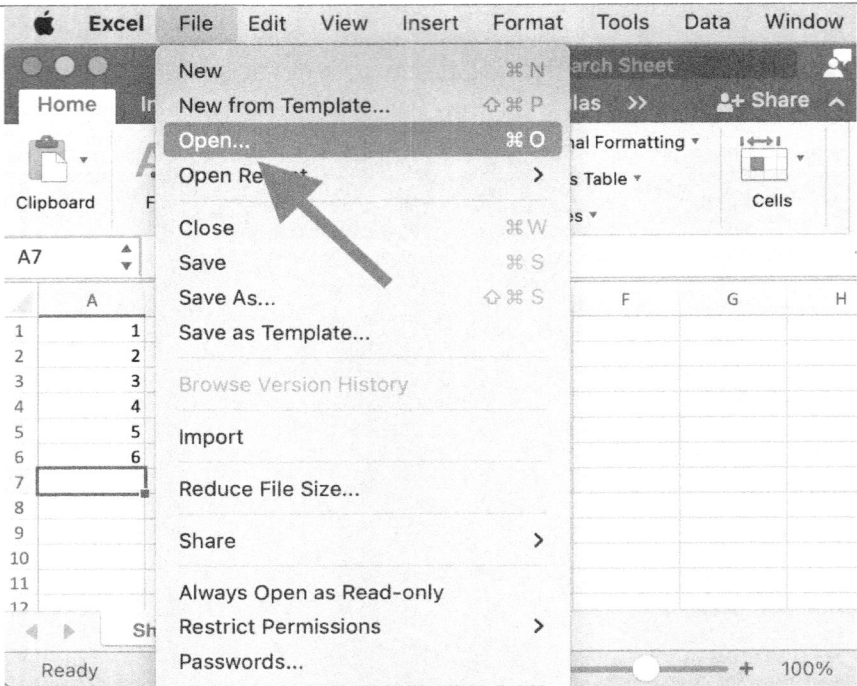

Browse to the folder where your workbook is stored.

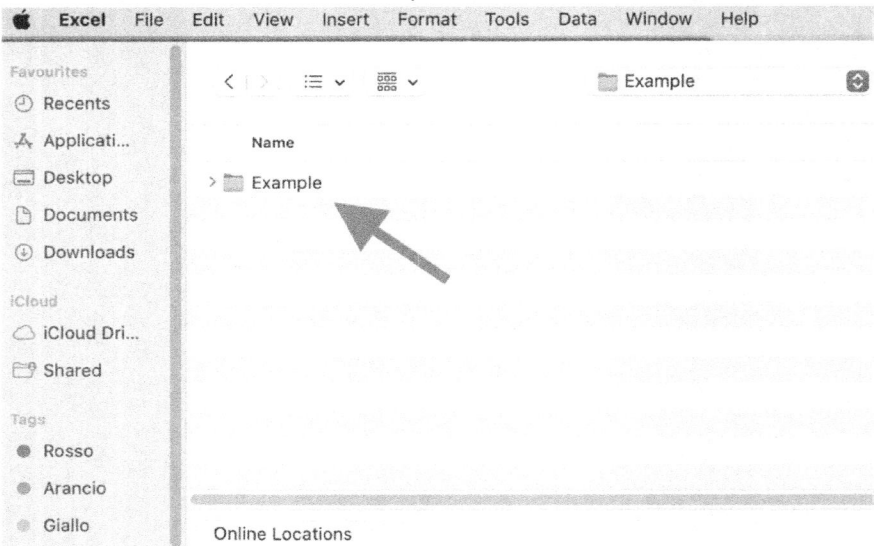

After selecting the appropriate file, click the "Open" button.

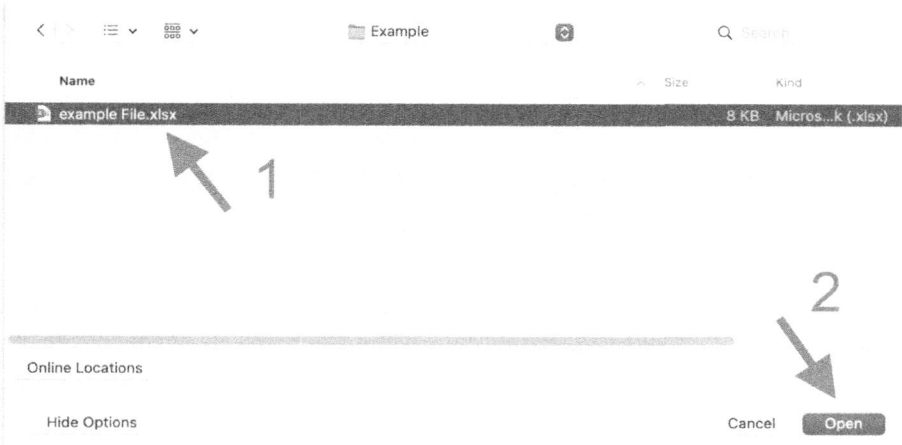

Alternatively, you may use the "Ctrl + O" keyboard shortcut to bring up the "Open" dialog box.

2.3.2 Closing a Workbook

One of the following approaches can be used to terminate a worksheet without quitting Excel:

Choose "Close" under the "File" option from the Ribbon.

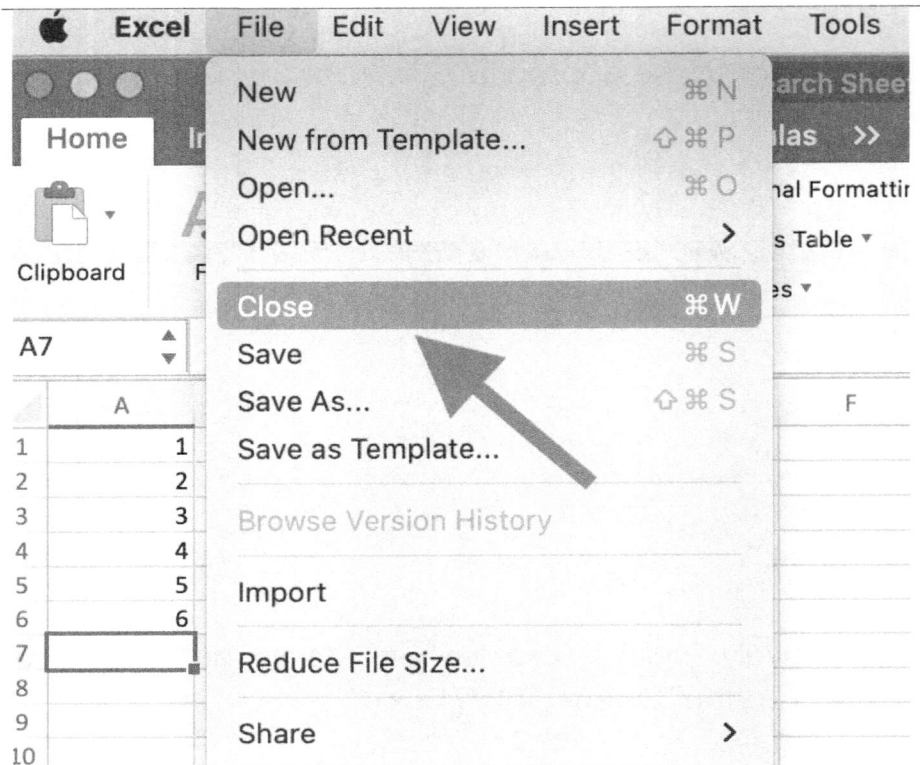

the keyboard's "Ctrl + W" key.

Excel will urge you to save your work before quitting the worksheet if there are any unsaved changes.

2.3.3 Renaming a Workbook

Use these procedures to rename an existing workbook:

Launch the worksheet that needs a new name.

EXCEL ESSENTIALS 2023

In the Ribbon, choose the "File" tab and select "Save As."

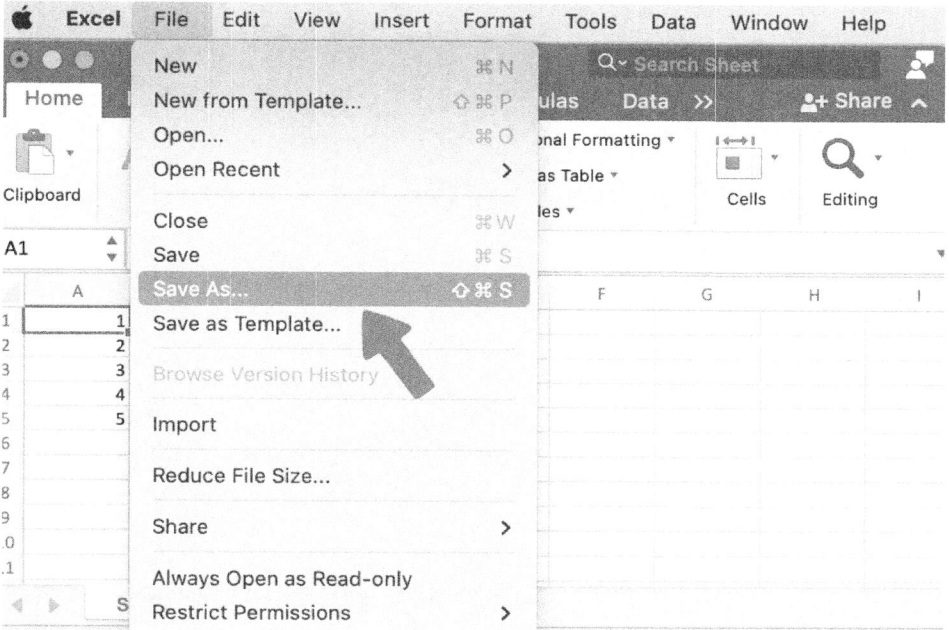

Select the file's current location.

In the "File name" box, type a new file name.

Select "Save" from the menu.

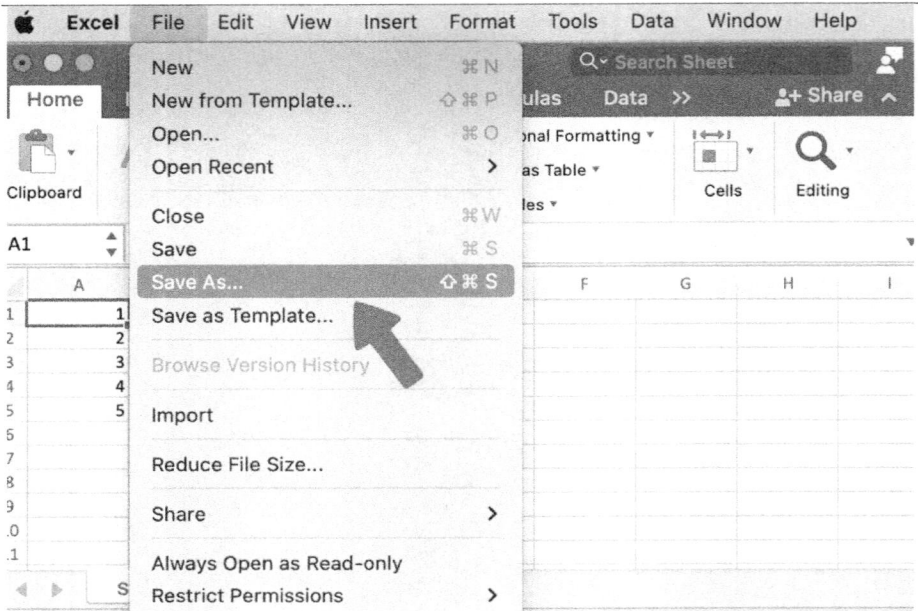

If preferred, you can delete the previous version of the workbook, and Excel will save a new copy with the modified file name.

You'll be well-equipped to operate effectively with Excel if you master these fundamental workbook creation and file management skills. The following chapters will go in-depth on the program's core features and capabilities to assist you in mastering the creation and manipulation of spreadsheets.

Chapter 3: Working with Cells, Rows, and Columns

3.1 Addressing and Cell References

Each cell in Excel has a specific address based on the row and column where it is located. A, B, C, and other letters denote the columns, whereas 1, 2, and so forth denote the rows. The combination of a cell's column letter and the row number is known as its address (for example, A1, B2, C3). Cell references are essential for formula creation, cell formatting, and effective spreadsheet navigation.

3.2 Choosing Rows, Columns, and Cells

You must first pick the cells, rows, or columns to enter data or take action on them. This is how you do it:

3.2.1 Picking Out Cells

To pick a single cell, click on it.

EXCEL ESSENTIALS 2023

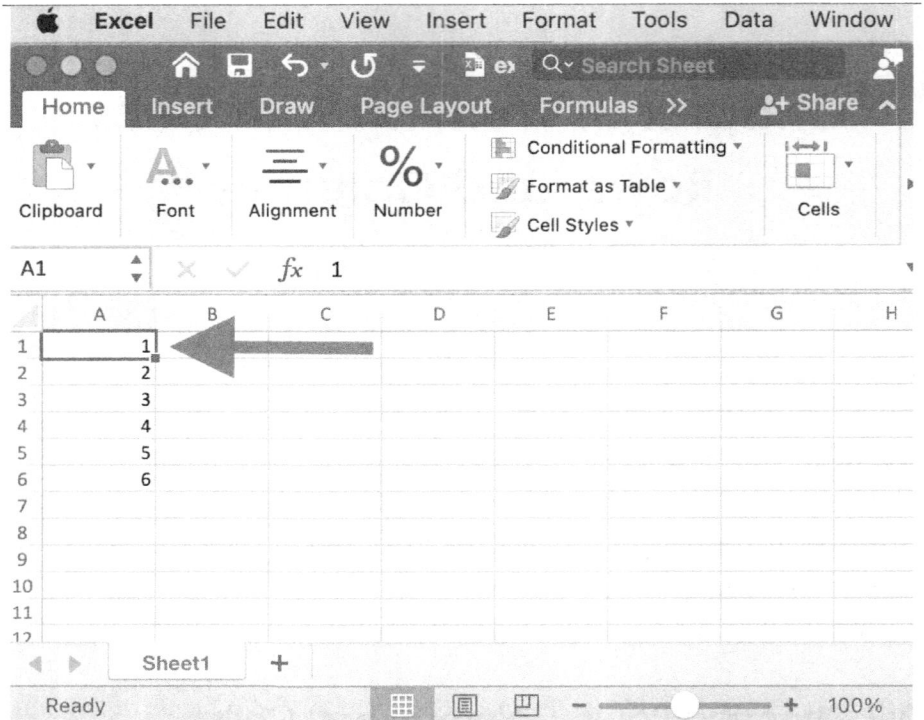

Simply click and drag your mouse over the required range to pick numerous neighboring cells.

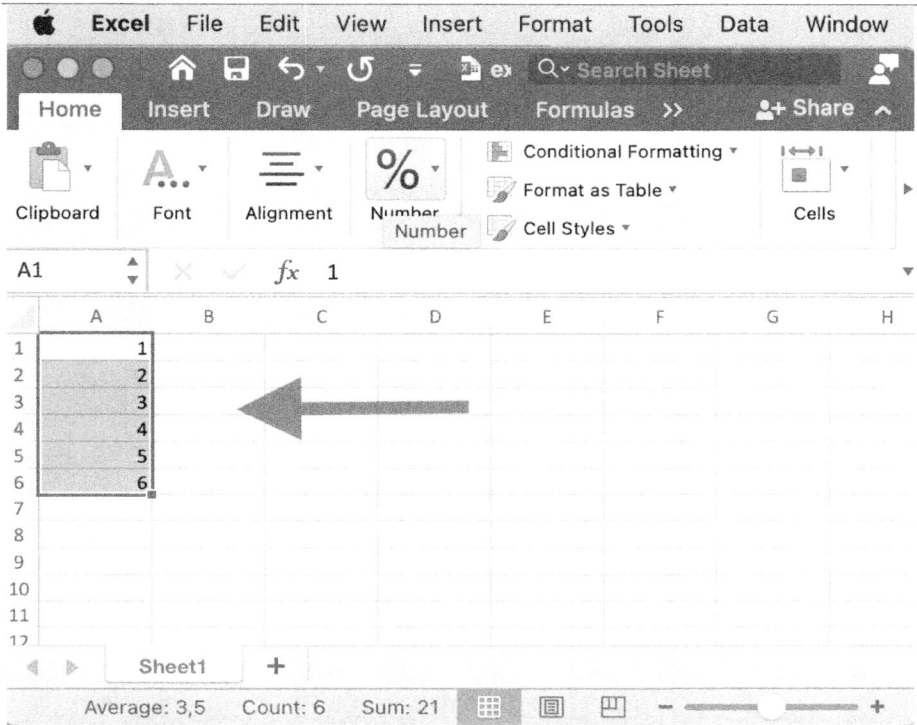

Hold down the "Ctrl" key while clicking on each cell you wish to choose to select non-adjacent cells.

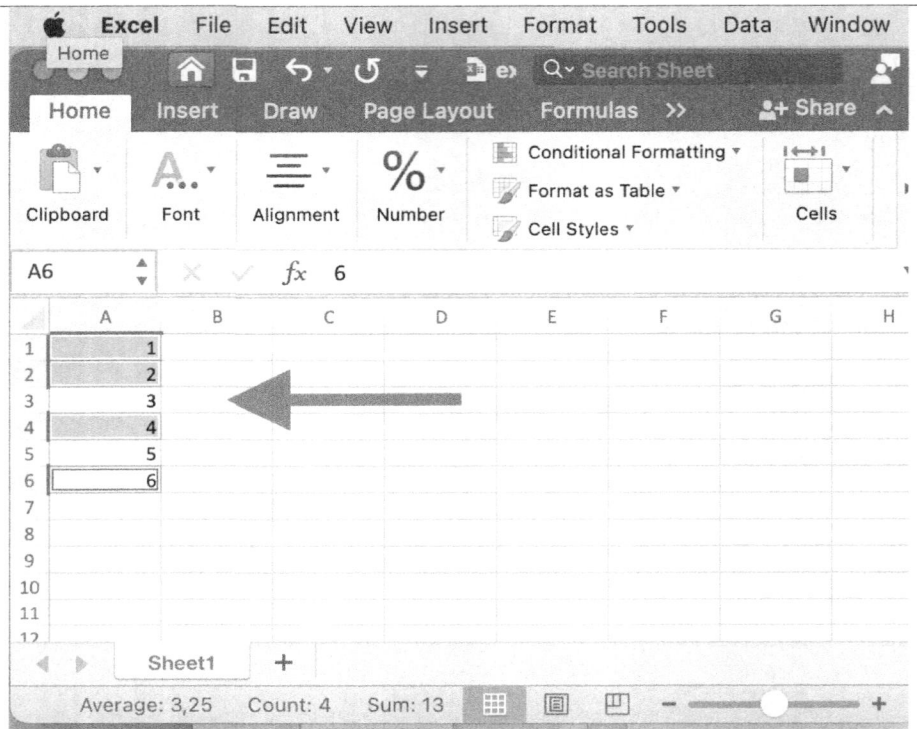

3.2.2 Choosing Columns and Rows

Click on the row number at the worksheet's left edge to pick a whole row.

EXCEL ESSENTIALS 2023

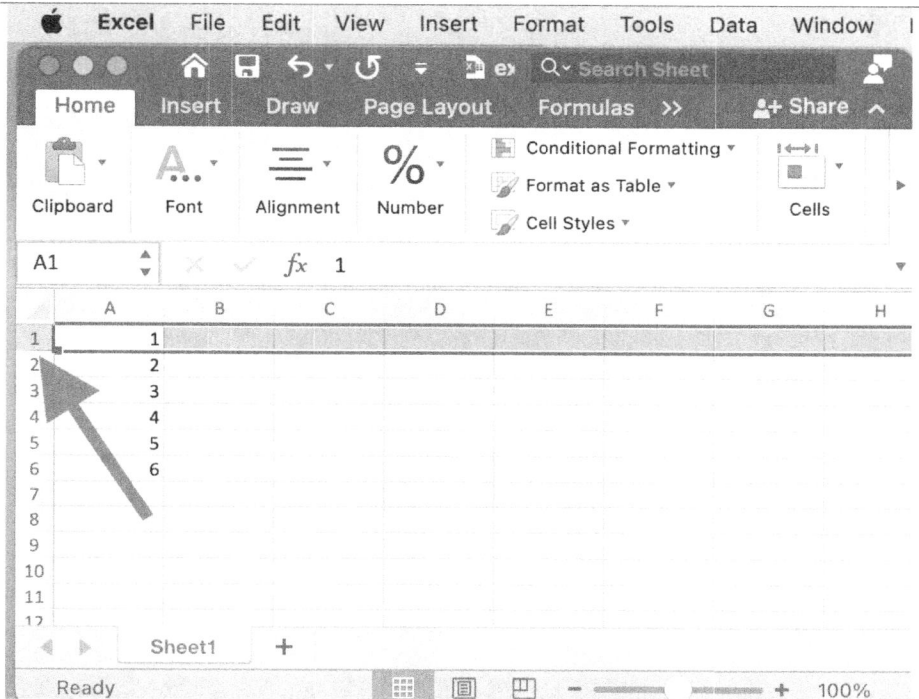

Click on the worksheet's column letter at the top to pick an entire column.

EXCEL ESSENTIALS 2023

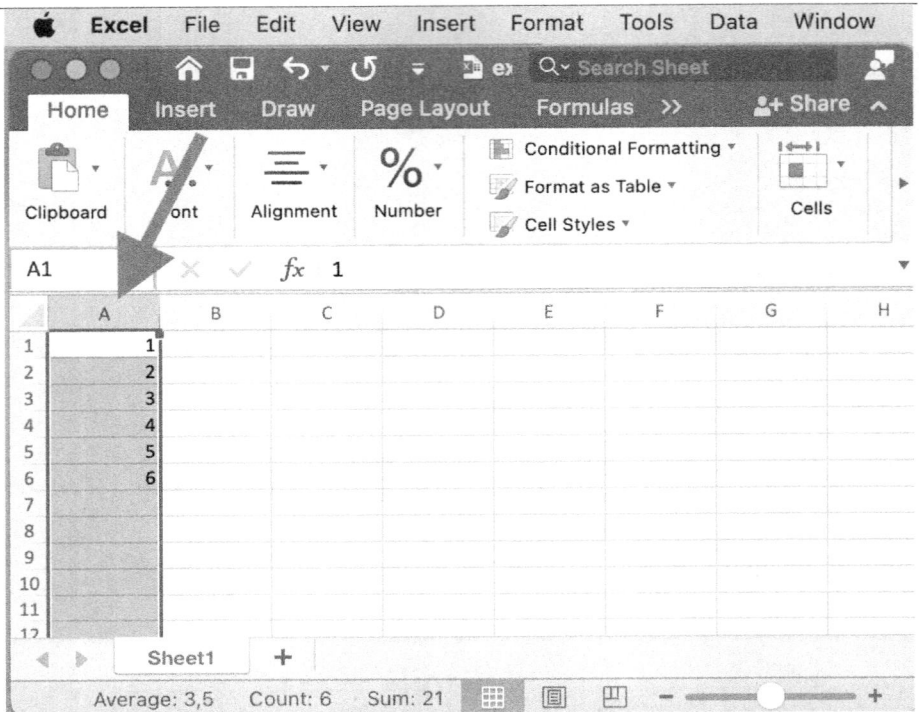

Click on the first row or column number or letter, then click and drag to highlight the required range to pick numerous neighboring rows or columns.

If you hold down the "Ctrl" key while clicking on each row number or column letter will allow you to choose non-adjacent rows or columns.

Follow the same procedure as outlined above (3.2.1 Picking Out Cells)

3.3 Adding and Removing Columns and Rows

You might need to add rows or columns or remove some as you work with your spreadsheet. This is how you do it:

3.3.1 Inserting Rows and Columns

Select the row above which you want to add a new row to insert it.

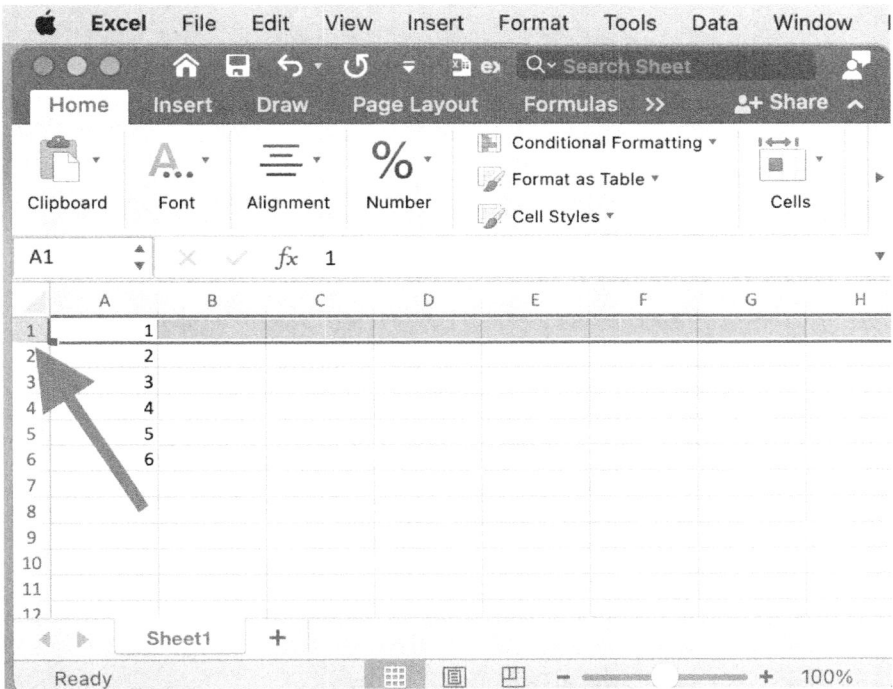

Select "Insert" from the context menu by right-clicking the row number.

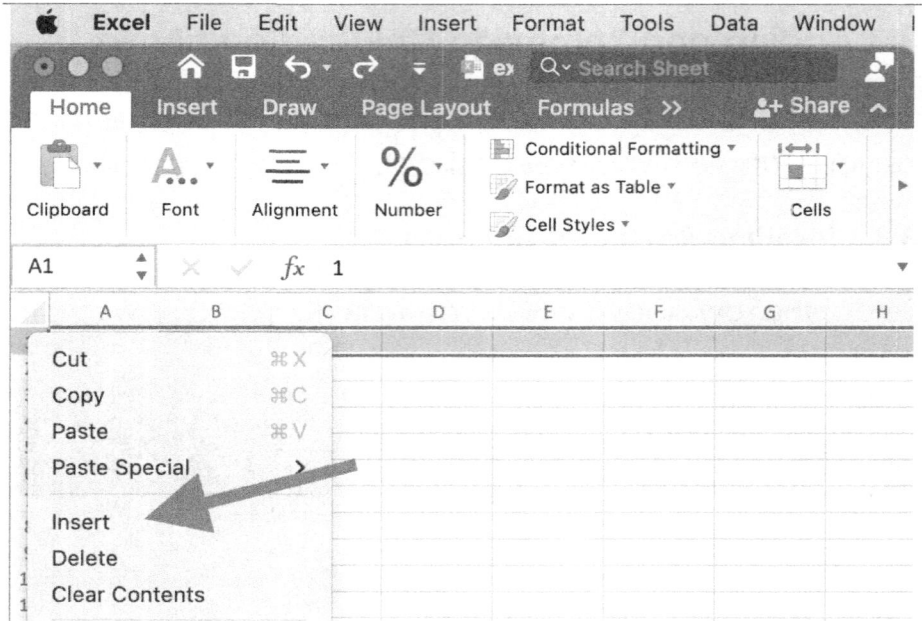

Select the column where you want the new column to appear on the left to insert it. Select "Insert" from the context menu by right-clicking the column letter.

The procedure is similar to the row entry procedure.

3.3.2 Removing Columns and Rows

Select the row you want to delete from the table to be deleted. Select "Delete" from the context menu by right-clicking the row number.

EXCEL ESSENTIALS 2023

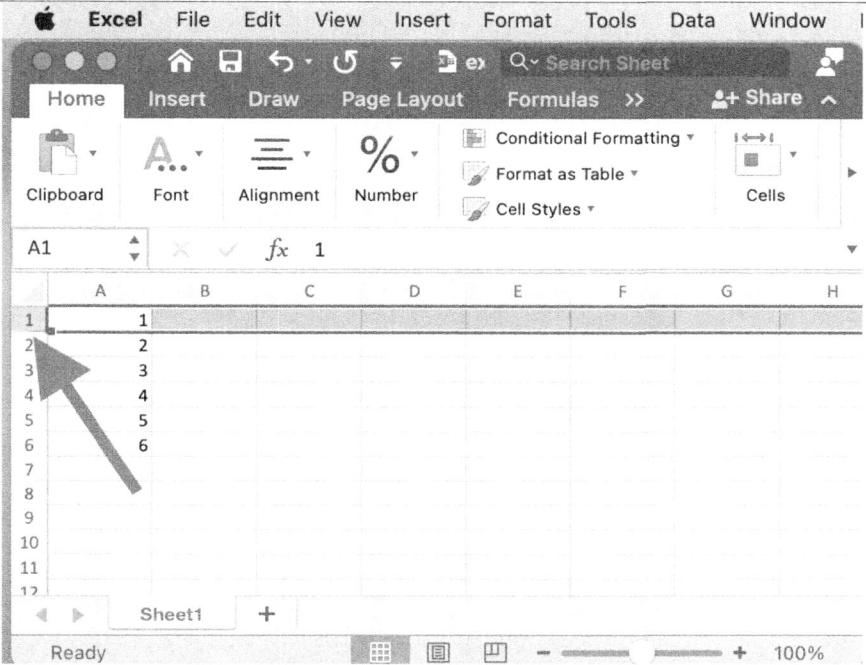

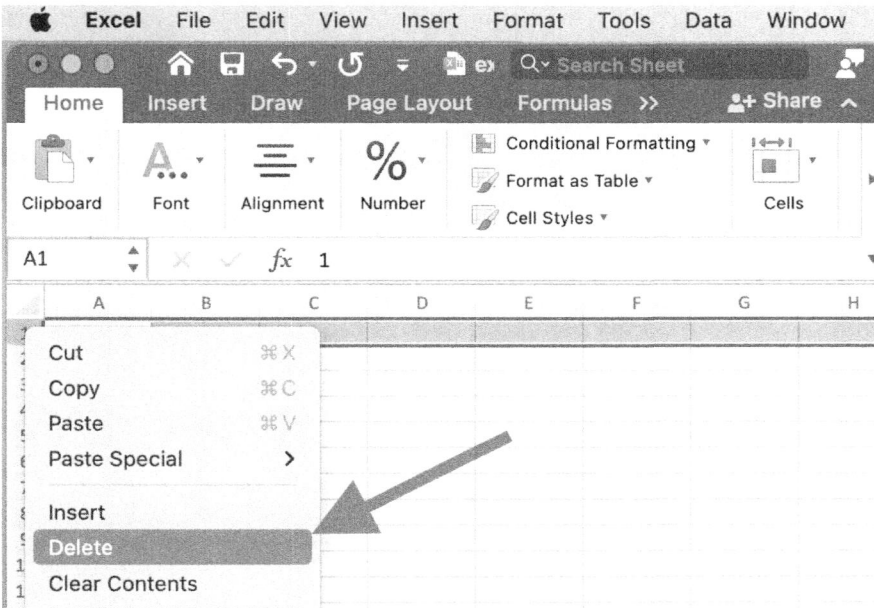

Select the column you wish to eliminate from the list. Select "Delete" from the context menu by right-clicking the column letter.

The procedure is similar to the row delete procedure.

3.4 Modifying Column Width and Row Height

Adjusting the row heights and column widths can enhance your spreadsheet's readability and look. This is how you do it:

3.4.1 Adjustment of Row Height

Click and drag the row number's bottom border up or down to change the height of a row manually.

Double-click the bottom edge of the row number to adjust the row to fit its content.

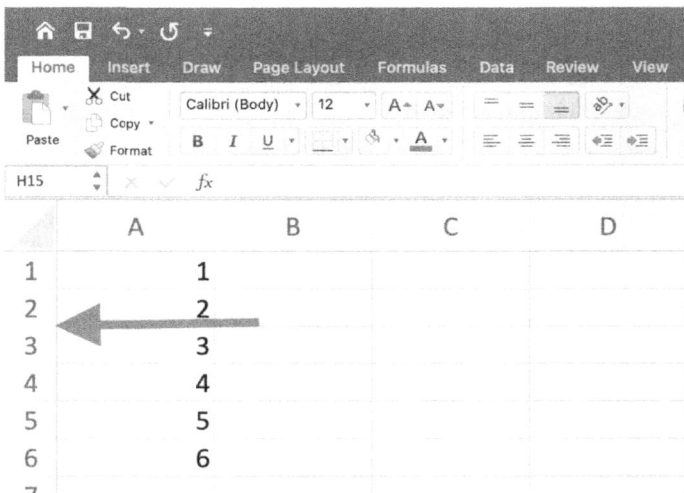

3.4.2 Adjusting Column Width

By clicking and dragging the right boundary of the column letter left or right, you may manually change the width of a column.

Double-click the right column letter border to adjust the column to fit its content automatically.

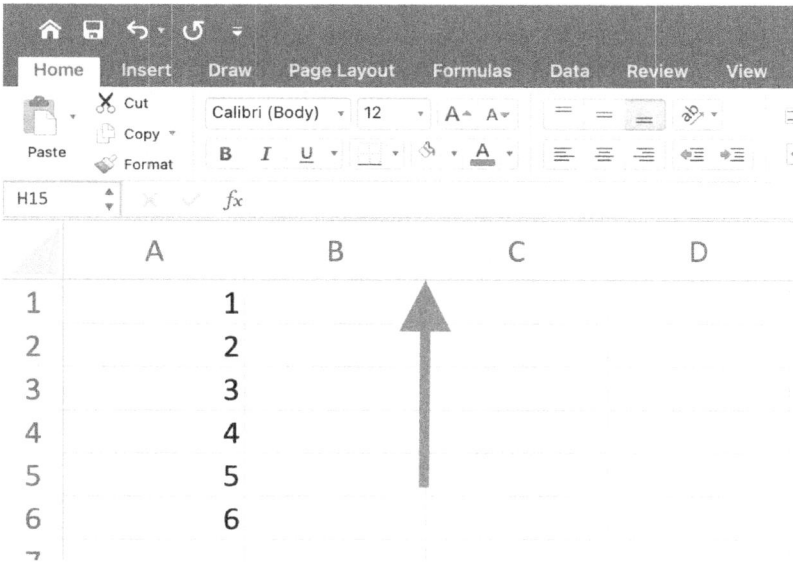

3.5 Cells that Merge and Unmerge

You can merge two or more neighboring cells into a single cell by merging them. This functionality is helpful when making headers, labels, or other items spanning numerous rows or columns. To combine and separate cells, adhere to these steps:

3.5.1 Cell Merging

The cells you wish to combine should be selected.

Select "Home" from the Ribbon tabs.

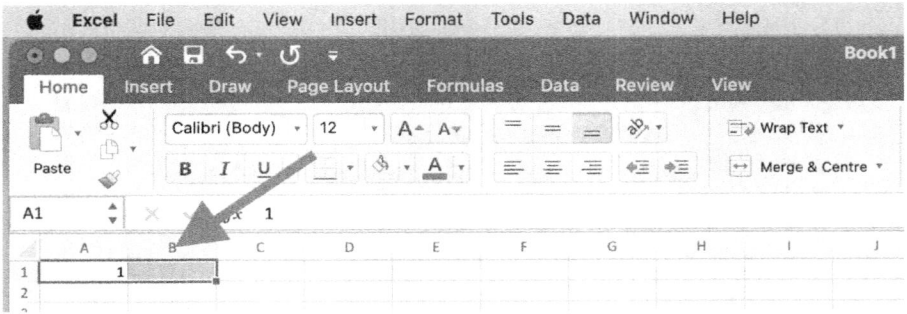

In the Alignment group, select the "Merge & Center" option.

To combine the cells and center the content, pick "Merge & Center" from the dropdown menu; alternatively, you may choose "Merge Cells" to merge the cells only.

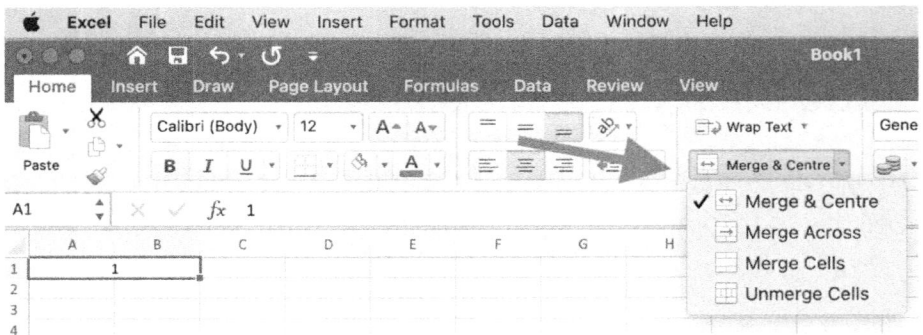

3.5.2 Unmerging Cells

To unmerge a merged cell, select it.

Select "Home" from the Ribbon tabs.

In the Alignment group, select the "Merge & Center" option.

From the dropdown menu, select "Unmerge Cells".

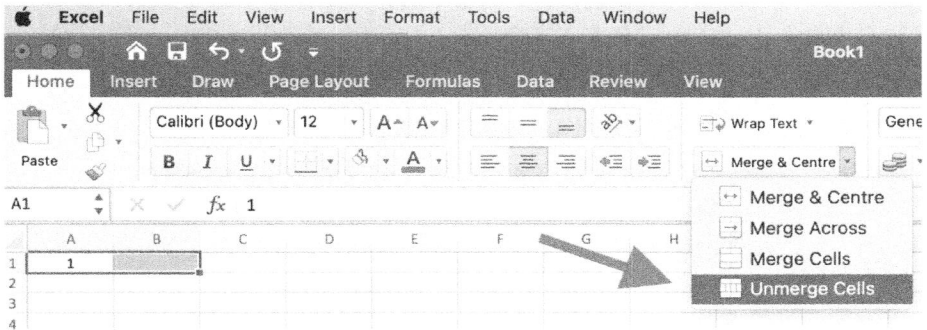

You are now prepared to begin inputting and formatting data into your spreadsheet now that you know how to deal with Excel's cells, rows, and columns. The following chapters will walk you through these steps and introduce you to crucial formulae and functions for handling your data.

Chapter 4: Entering and Formatting Data

4.1 Text and Number Entry

Excel makes it easy to enter data by simply selecting a cell and entering the required information. To insert text and numbers, follow these steps:

Input data into the cell by clicking on it.

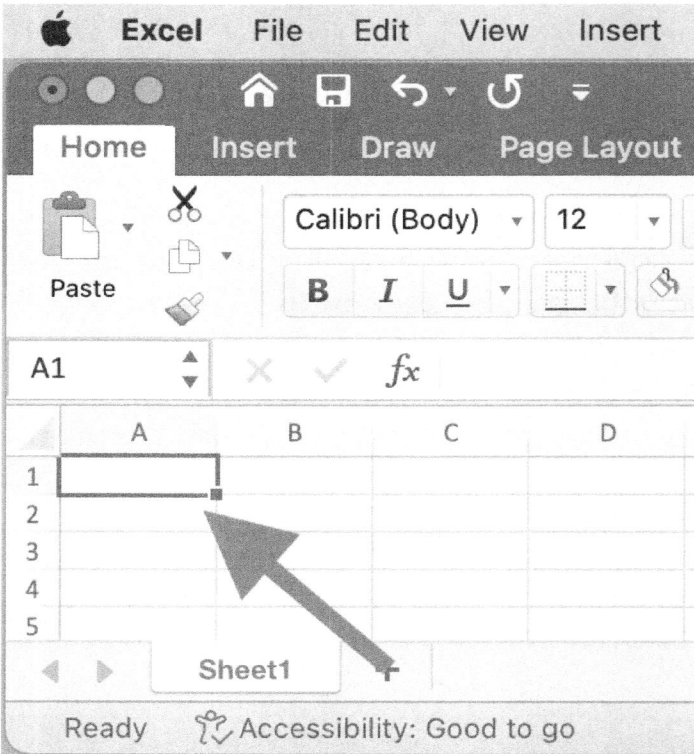

Type the text or numbers directly into the cell.

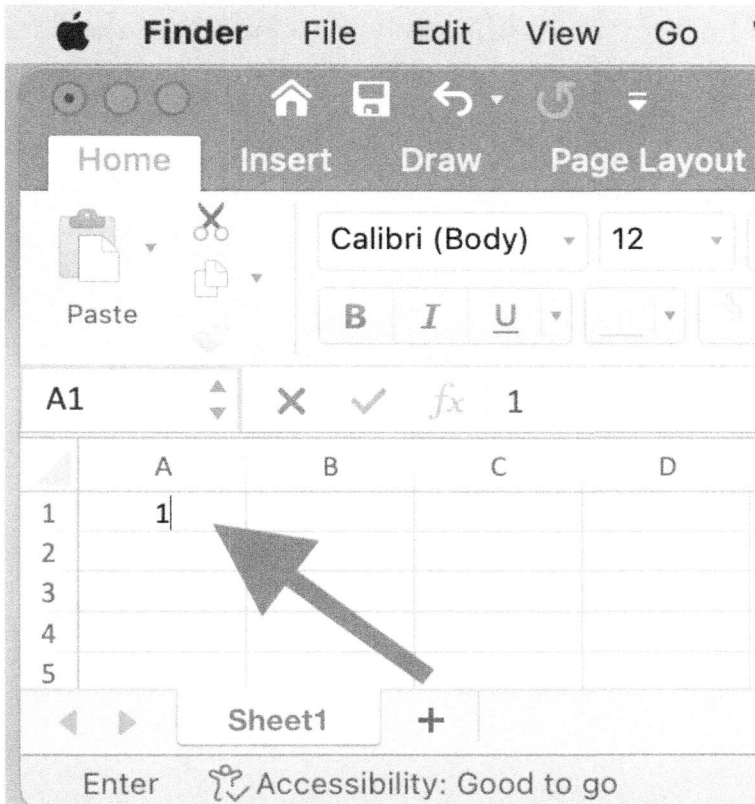

You can hit "Tab" to go to the right or "Enter" to confirm your entry and advance to the following cell.

When completing calculations, remember that Excel differs between text and numbers, so ensure you enter data in the proper format.

4.2 Formatting Cells

Your spreadsheet's readability and look can be improved by formatting the cells. Formatting choices in Excel include font style, size, color, and alignment. The following describes how to format cells simply:

4.2.1 Size, Color, and Font

Choose the cell(s) that need formatting.

Select "Home" from the ribbon tabs.

Use the dropdown options in the Font group to pick a font, size, or color for your selected cells.

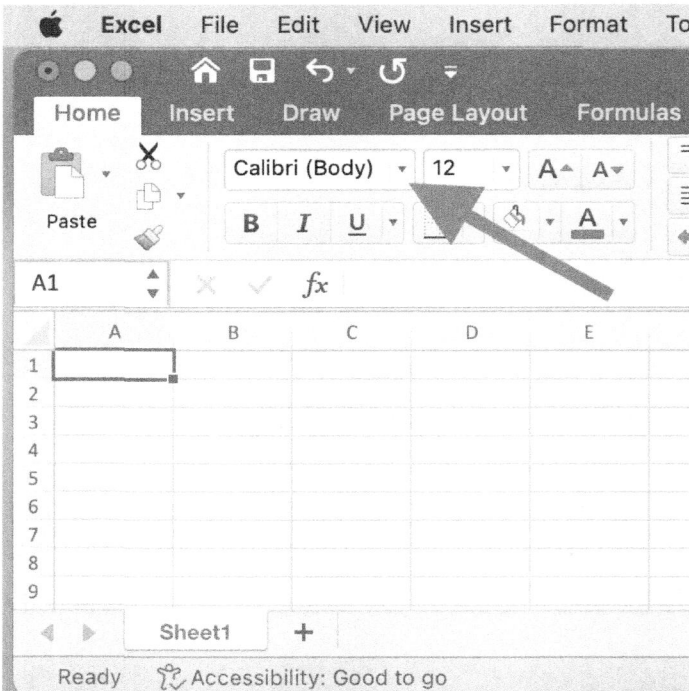

EXCEL ESSENTIALS 2023

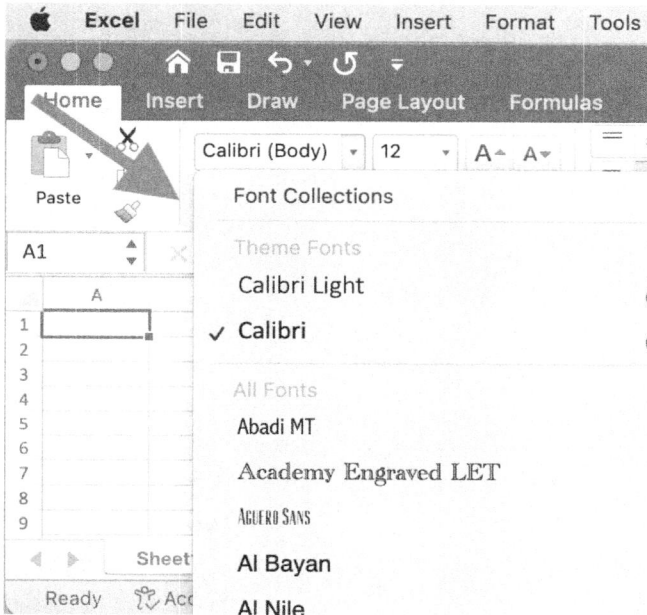

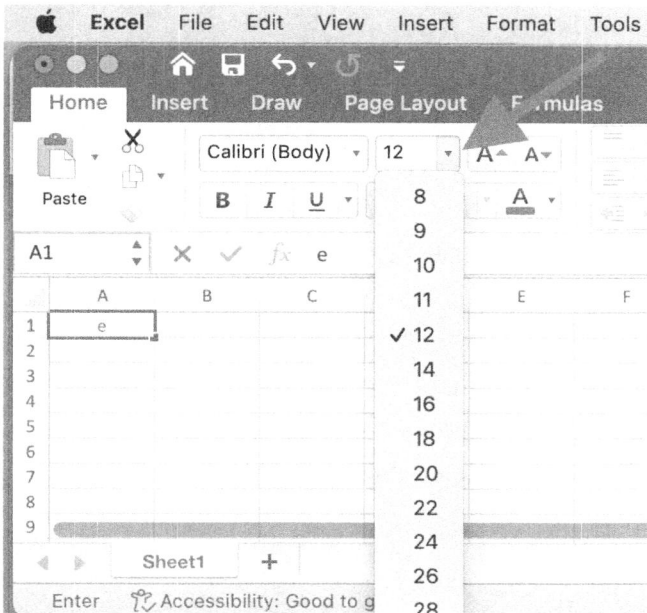

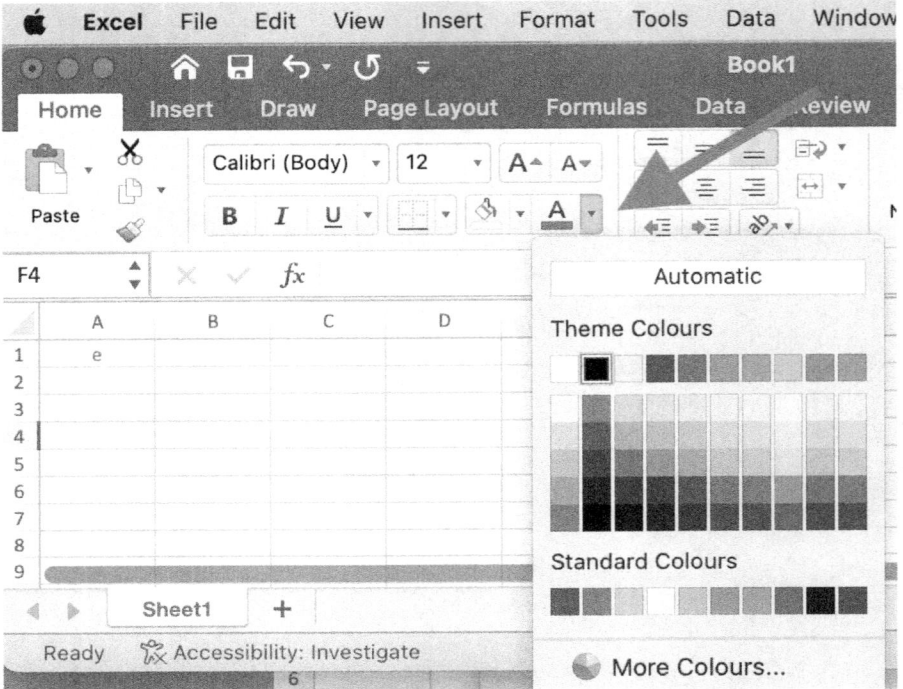

4.2.2 Linearity

Pick the cell or cells that you want to align.

Select "Home" from the ribbon tabs.

To change the horizontal alignment, click one of the alignment buttons (left, center, or right) in the Alignment group. To change the vertical alignment, select one of the alignment buttons (top, middle, or bottom).

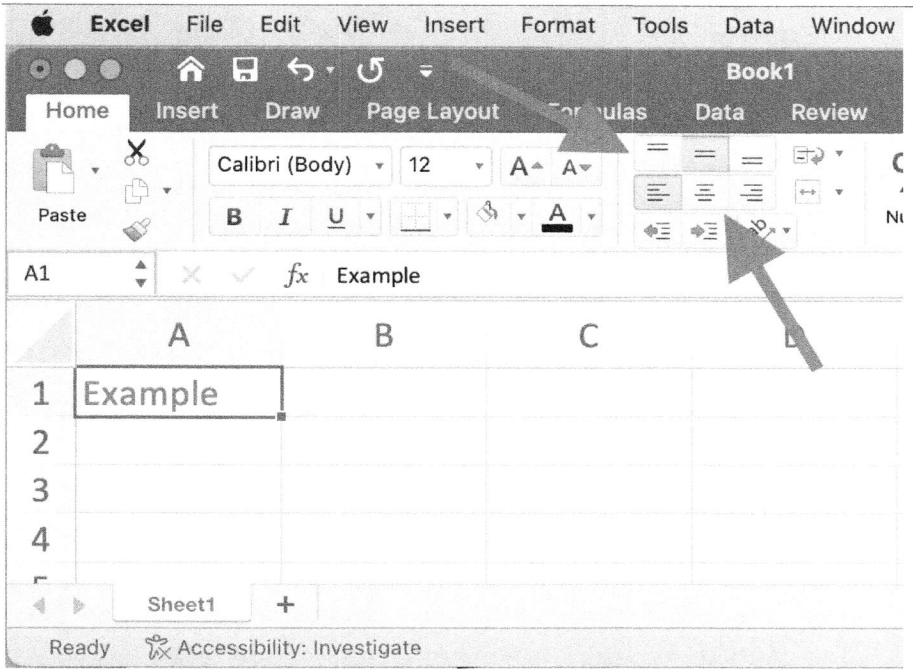

4.3 Applying Number Formats

How numerical data is displayed in your spreadsheet is controlled by number formats. There are many number formats available in Excel, including currency, percentage, date, and time, are available in Excel. How to insert a number format into a cell is shown here:

Choose the cell or cells that contain the numbers you wish to format.

Select "Home" from the ribbon tabs.

EXCEL ESSENTIALS 2023

Use the drop-down menu in the Number group to pick a number format for your chosen cells.

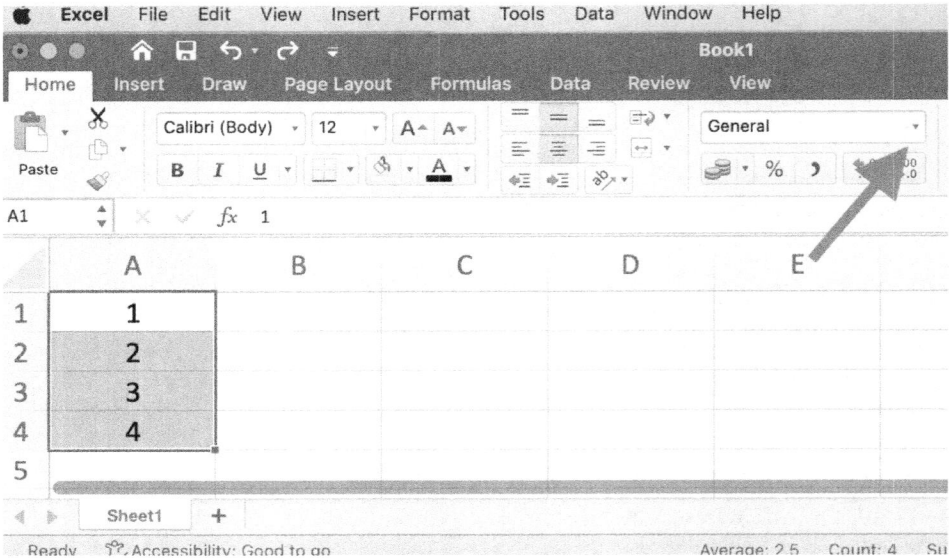

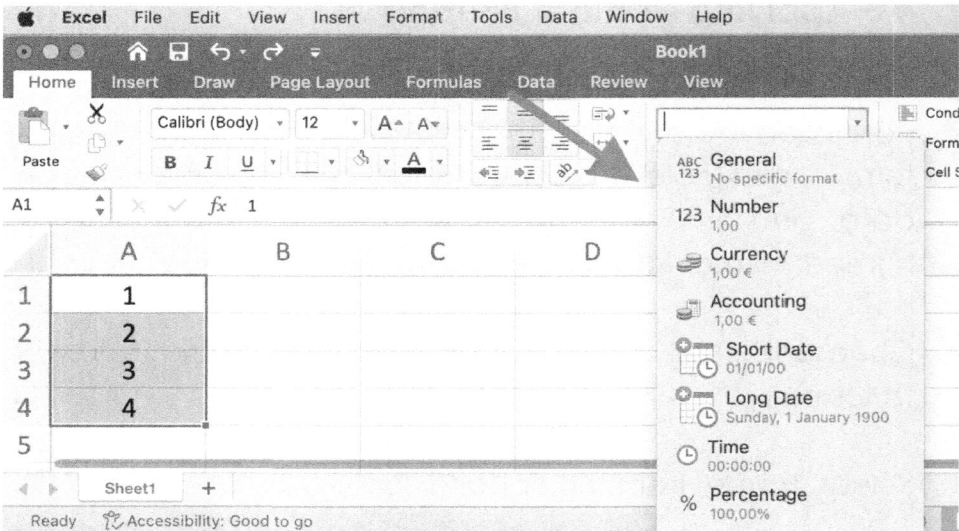

4.4 Making Use of Border and Fill Colors

Applying borders and fill colors to your spreadsheet may aid data organization, emphasize essential information, and enhance visual appeal. Here's how to provide cells borders and color fills:

4.4.1 Addition of Borders

Choose the cell(s) to which boundaries should be added.

Select "Home" from the ribbon tabs.

Select the "Borders" button (seen as a square with grid lines in the Font group).

From the dropdown menu, select a border style, such as "All Borders," "Thick Box Border," or "Top and Bottom Borders."

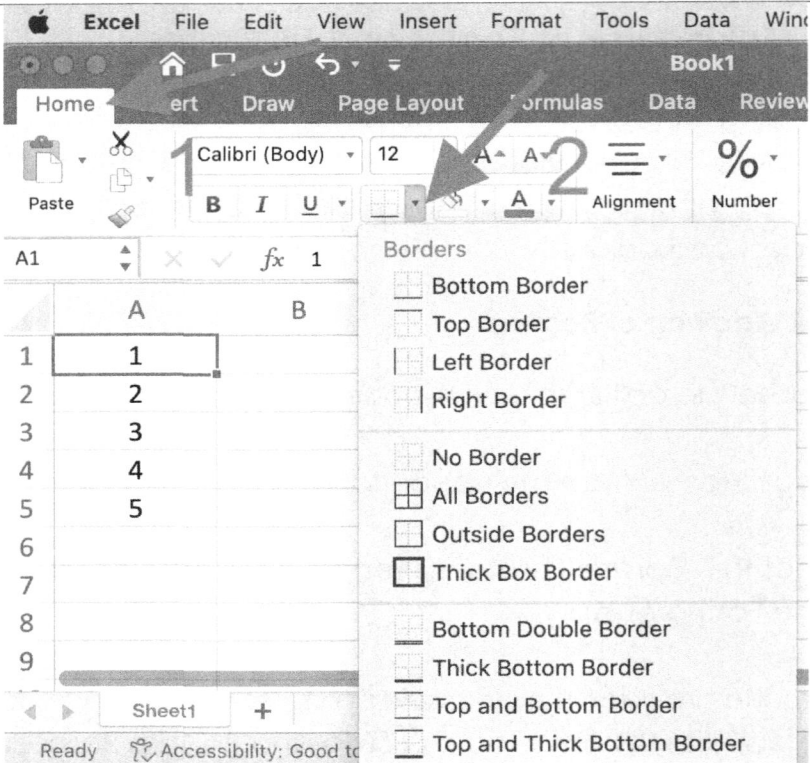

4.4.2 Applying to Fill Colors

Choose the cell(s) you wish to add a fill color to.

Select "Home" from the ribbon tabs.

Select the "Fill Color" button (shown as a paint bucket icon) in the Font group.

Select a color from the drop-down menu, or click "More Colors" for more choices.

EXCEL ESSENTIALS 2023

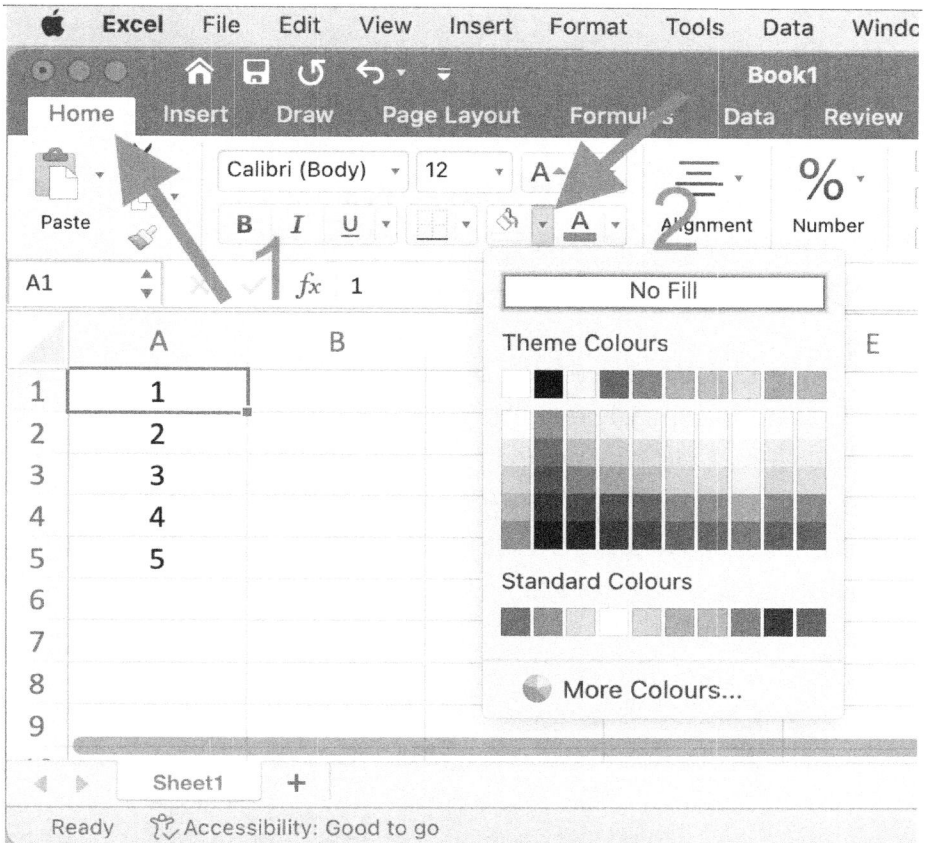

You are now prepared to begin creating your spreadsheets because you have mastered the fundamentals of data entry and formatting. The following chapters will teach you how to build formulae and functions, sort and filter data, and use charts and graphs to represent your data.

Chapter 5: Basic Formulas and Functions

5.1 Developing Basic Formulas

You may do calculations and change the data in your spreadsheet using formulas in Excel. Follow these steps to generate a straightforward formula:

Select the cell where you wish the calculation's outcome to appear by clicking there.

To indicate that you are entering a formula, type the equal symbol (=).

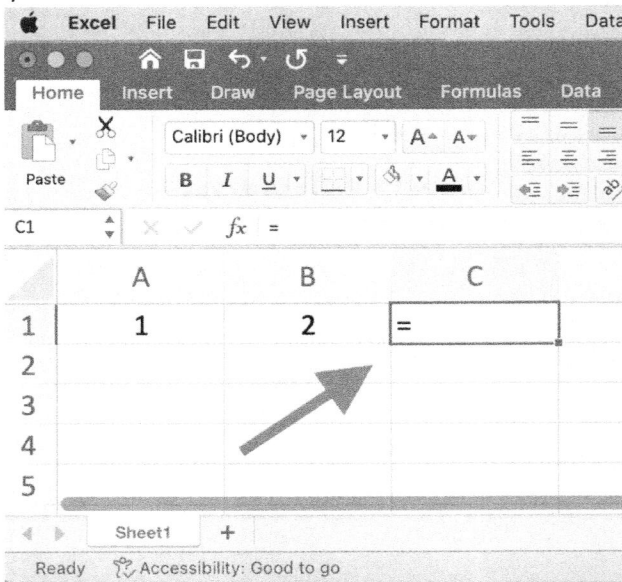

Enter the formula using cell references and the (+, -, *, /) arithmetic operators. To combine cells A1 and B1, for instance, type "=A1+B1."

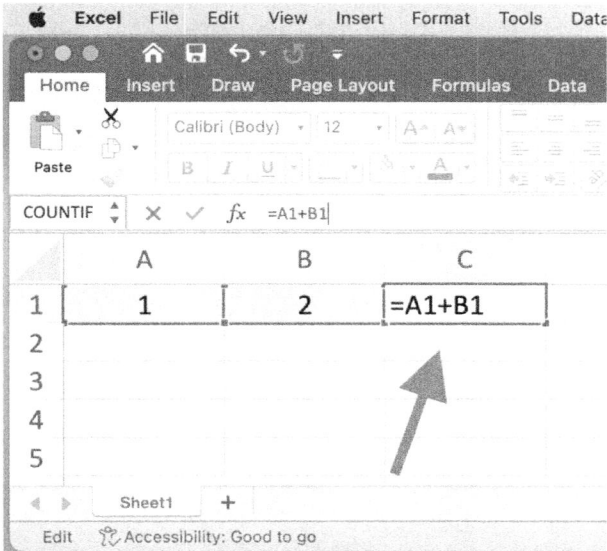

EXCEL ESSENTIALS 2023

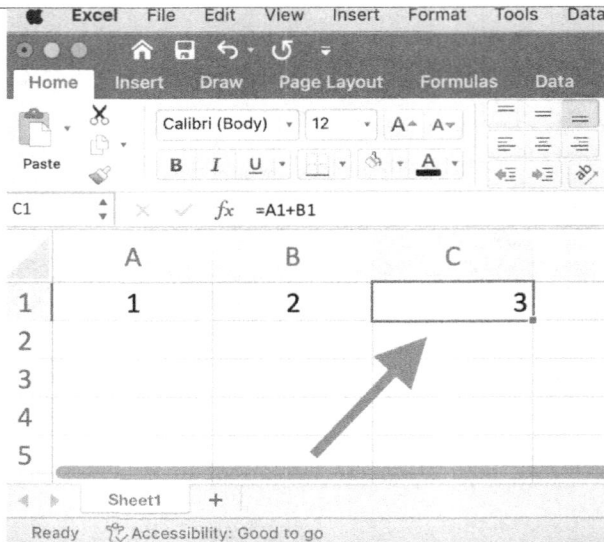

To display the formula and result, press "Enter" once.

5.2 Using Foundational Features

In Excel, functions are preset formulae that carry out certain computations or tasks. They can speed up computations and make them simpler. The following are some fundamental operations and how to use them:

5.2.1 SUM Function

A numeric range can be added up using the SUM function. Follow these steps to utilize the SUM function:

The cell where you wish the total to display should be clicked.

To begin using the function, type =SUM(.

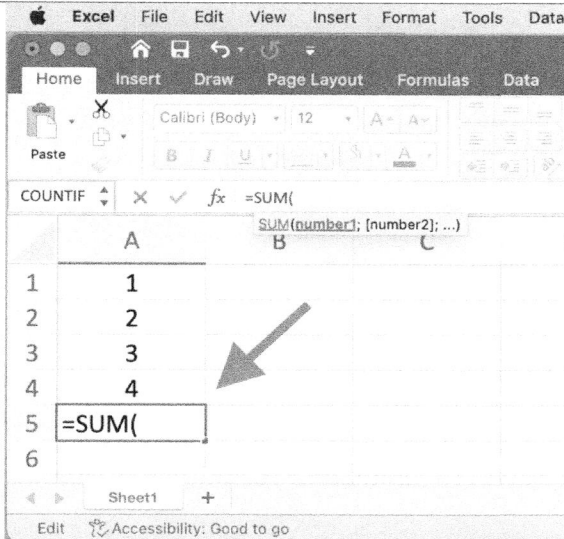

Choose the range of cells you wish to add or write the cell references (for example, A1:A4 or A1, B1, C1) with commas between each reference.

Press "Enter" after closing the function with a parenthesis).

Enter =SUM(A1:A4) to obtain the sum of the integers in cells A1 to A4.

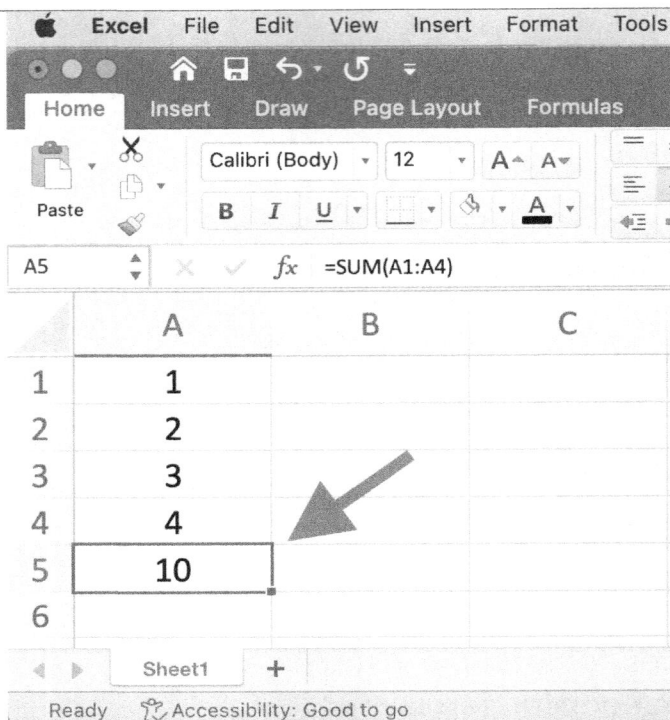

5.2.2 AVERAGE Function

The average of a range of numbers is determined using the AVERAGE function. These steps should be followed to use the AVERAGE function:

The cell where you wish the average to appear should be clicked.

To begin the function, type =AVERAGE(.

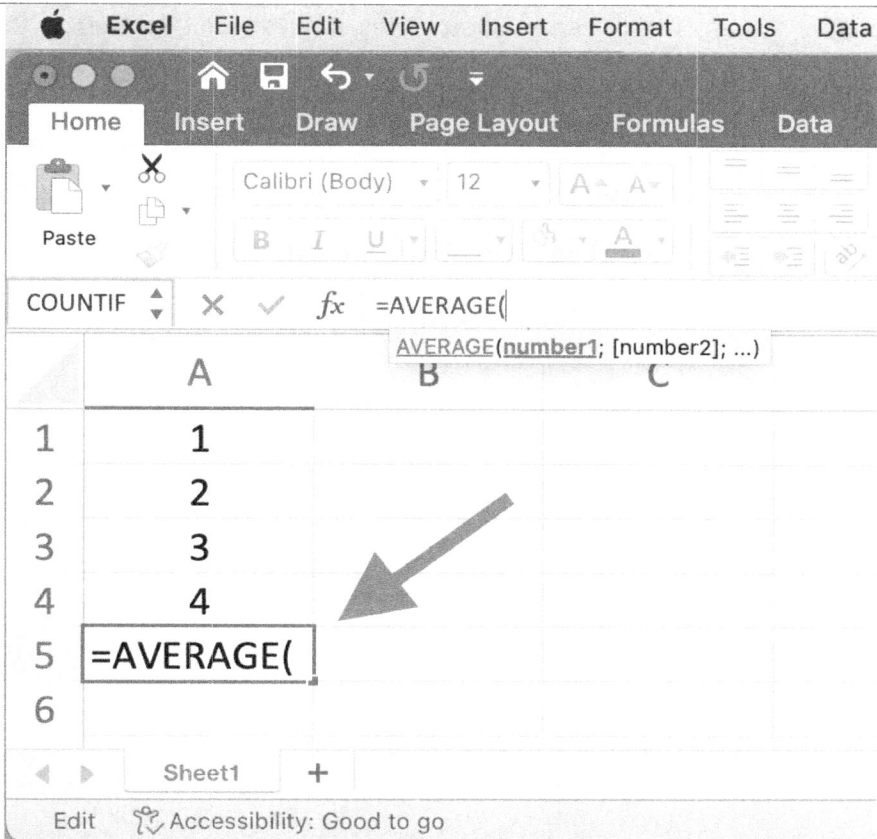

Choose the range of cells you wish to average, or enter the comma-separated cell references.

Press "Enter" after closing the function with a parenthesis).

through obtain the average of the numbers in cells A1 through A4, for instance, type "=AVERAGE(A1:A4)."

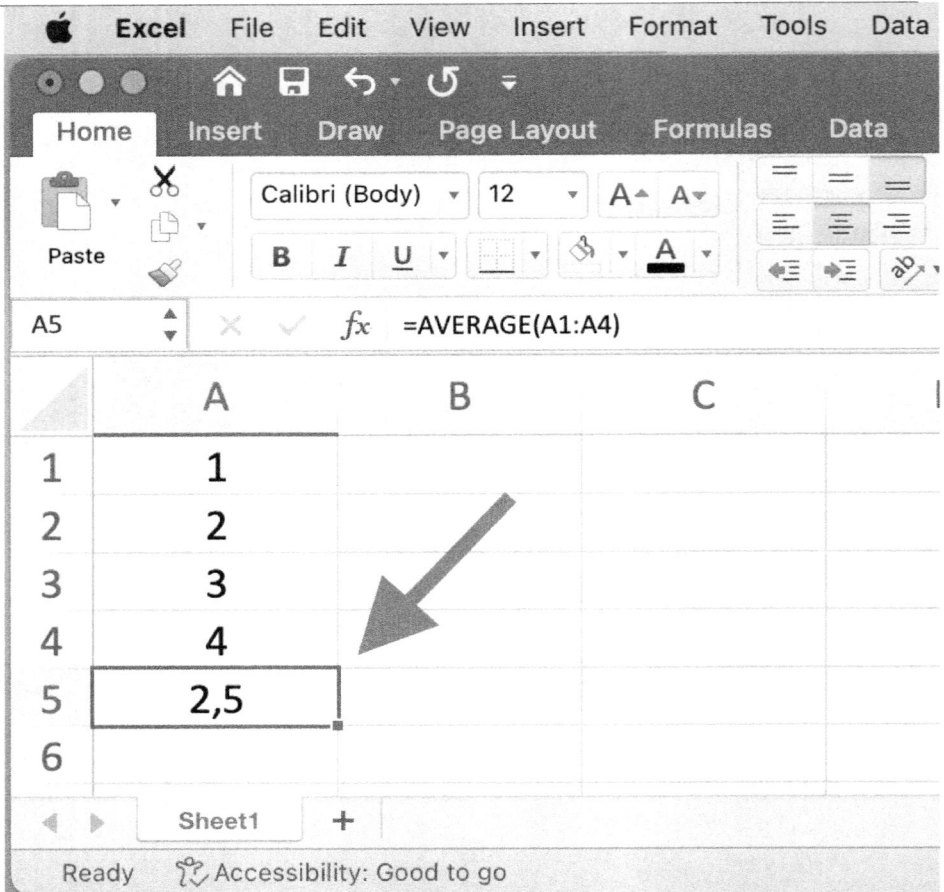

5.2.3 Function of COUNT

The COUNT function counts the number of cells in a range that contain numerical data. These steps should be followed to utilize the COUNT function:

The cell where you wish the count to display should be clicked.

EXCEL ESSENTIALS 2023

To invoke the function, type =COUNT(.

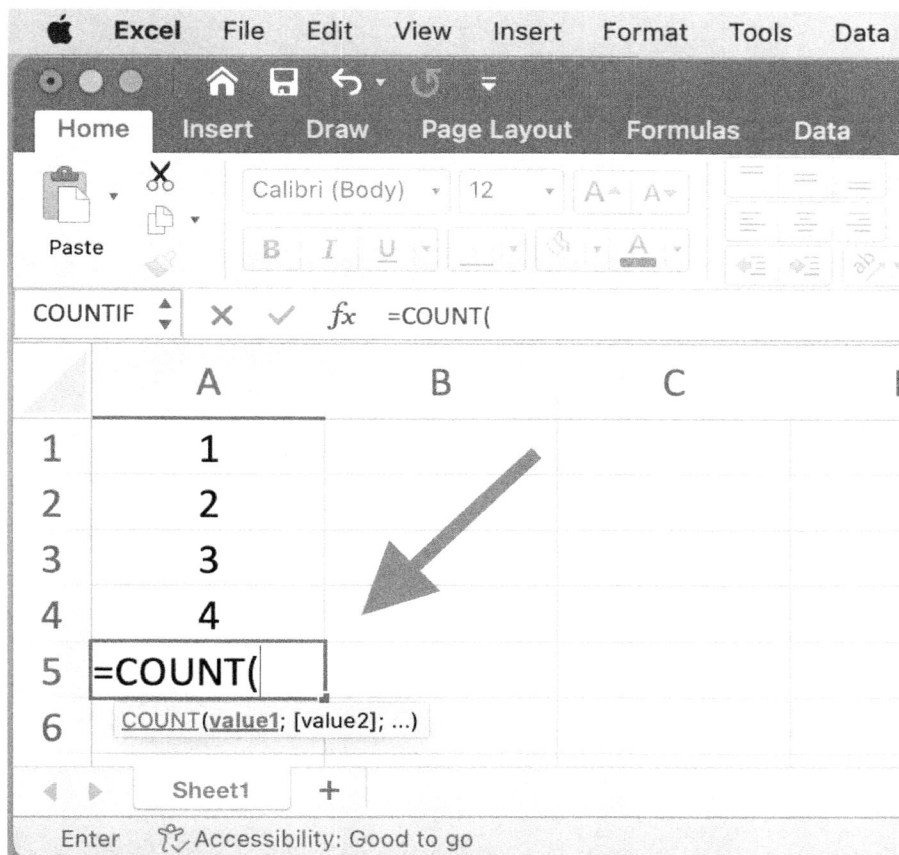

Choose the cells you wish to count or type the cell references with commas between each one.

Press "Enter" after closing the function with a parenthesis).

For instance, use "=COUNT(A1:A4)" to count the number of cells in cells A1 through A4 that contain numbers.

| | Excel | File | Edit | View | Insert | Format | Tools | Data |

Home   Insert   Draw   Page Layout   Formulas   Data

Calibri (Body) ▾ 12 ▾ A▴ A▾

B I U ▾

Paste

A5 fx =COUNT(A1:A4)

	A	B	C	[
1	1			
2	2			
3	3			
4	4			
5	4			
6				

Sheet1   +

Ready   Accessibility: Good to go

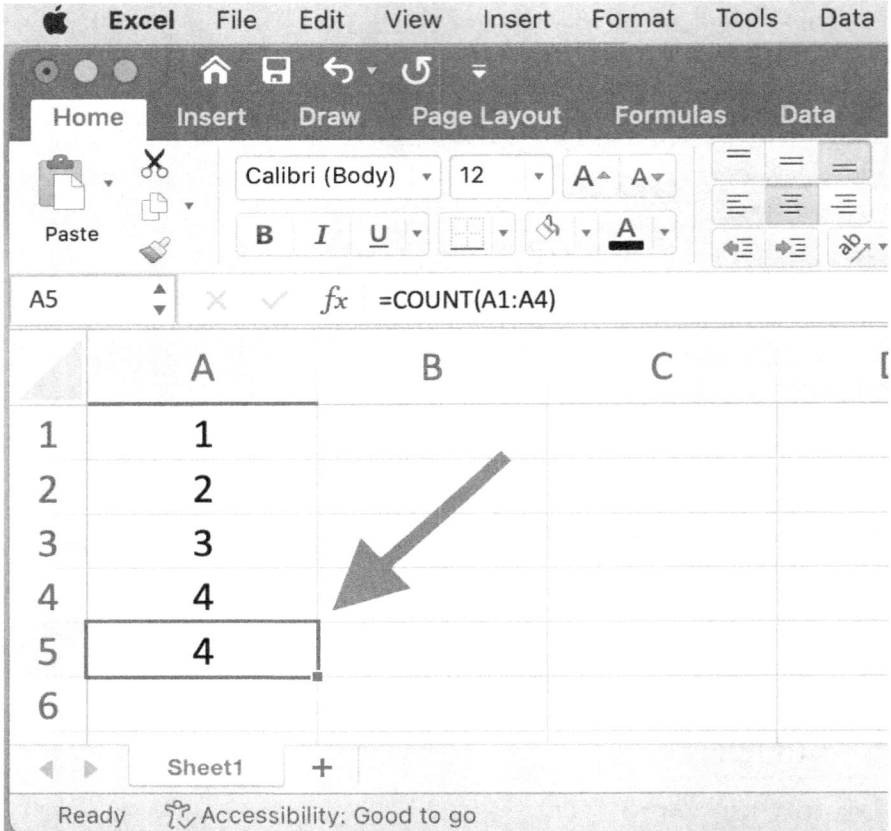

5.3 Understanding Relative and Absolute Cell References

If a formula's cell references are absolute or relative, they could change when you copy and paste it into Excel:

When you copy and paste a formula, relative cell references (such as A1) immediately change. For instance, if you duplicate a formula from cell B1 to B2, A1 will now link to cell A2, not cell B1.

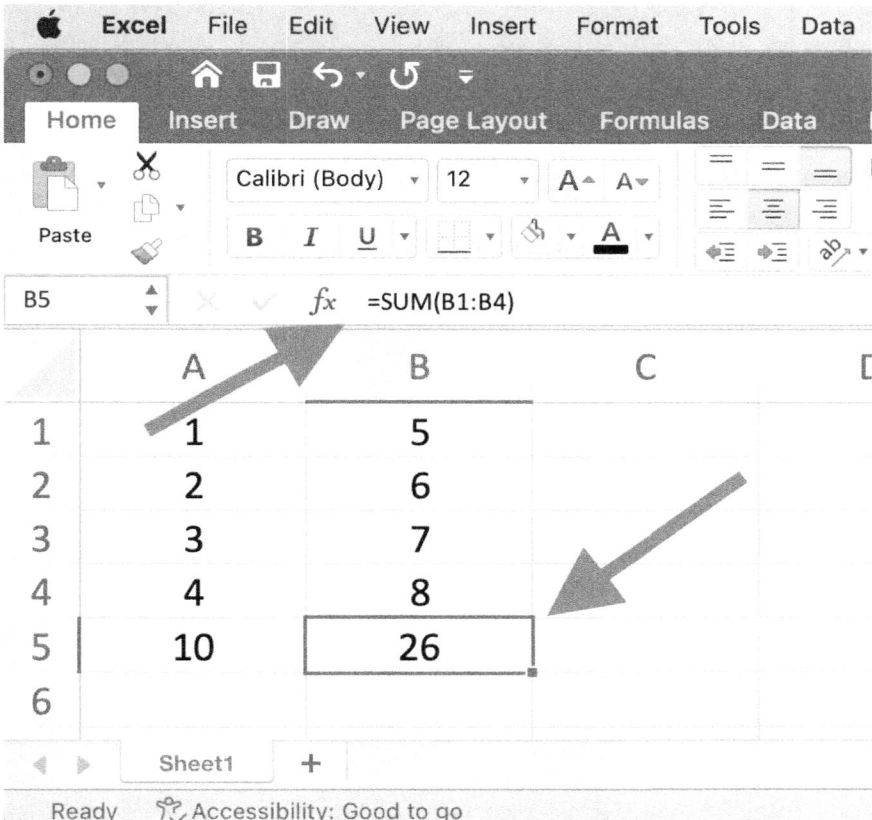

When you copy and paste a formula, absolute cell references (such as $A$1) don't change. For instance, the reference to $A$1 will remain the same if you transfer a formula from cell B1 to cell B2.

EXCEL ESSENTIALS 2023

Press the "F4" key while formula editing to change the cell references between relative and absolute.

EXCEL ESSENTIALS 2023

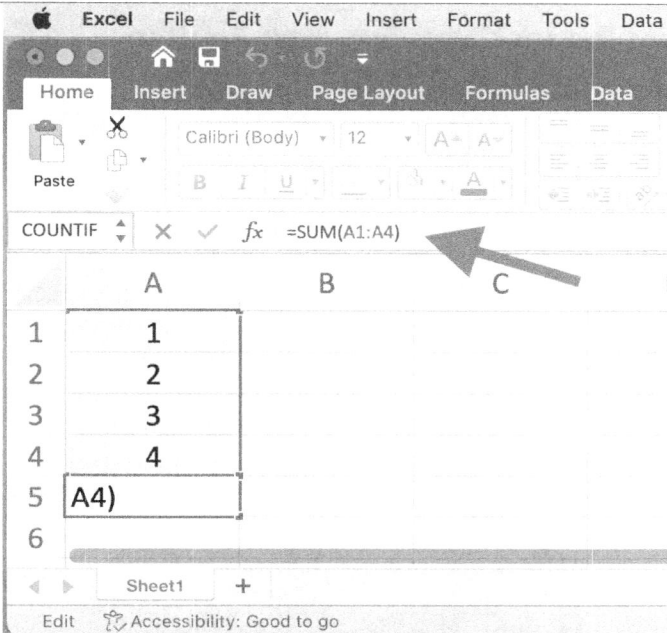

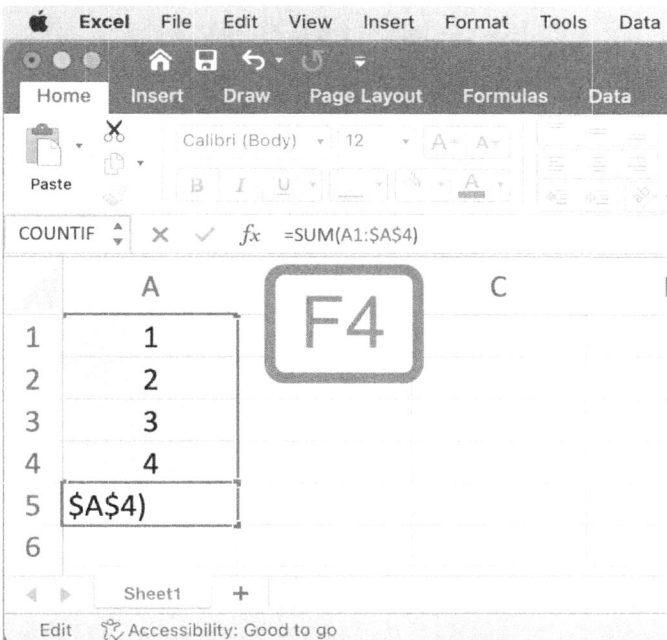

5.4 Formulas for Copying and Pasting

Once a formula has been established, you may copy and paste it into more cells for the same computation. This is how you do it:

The cell holding the formula you wish to duplicate should be selected.

Click the "Copy" button in the Clipboard group on the Home tab, or press "Ctrl + C" on your keyboard.

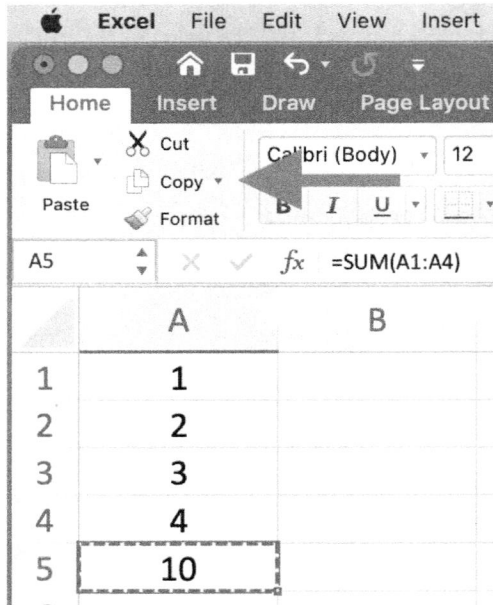

Choose the cells you wish to put the formula into.

In the Clipboard group on the Home tab, click the "Paste" button or press "Ctrl + V" on your keyboard.

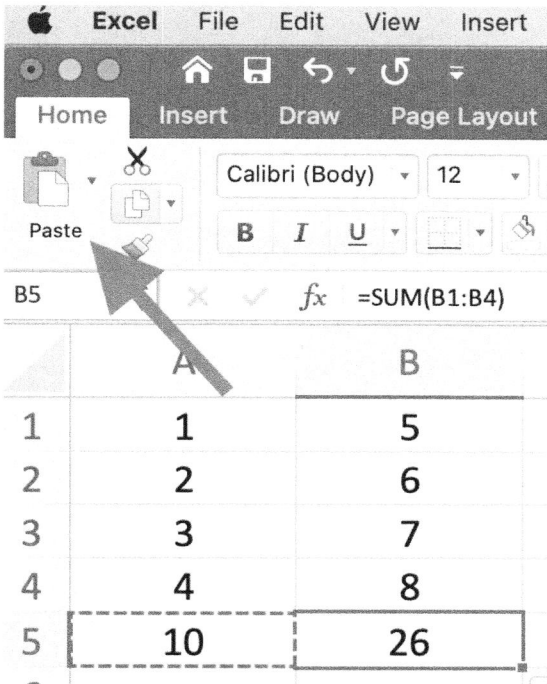

Remember that relative cell references will change automatically when copying a formula, but absolute cell references will not.

Now that you know these basic formulas and functions, you can use Excel more effectively to conduct computations and analyze data. In the following chapters, you'll discover how to construct charts and graphs, sort and filter data, and prepare your spreadsheet for printing.

Chapter 6: Sorting and Filtering Data

6.1 Data Sorting by One or More Columns

By sorting the data, you may arrange your spreadsheet depending on particular criteria, such as alphabetical order, numerical values, or dates. Data can be sorted by a single column or numerous columns in Excel. This is how you do it:

6.1.1 Sorting by a Single Column

In the column you wish to sort, choose a cell.

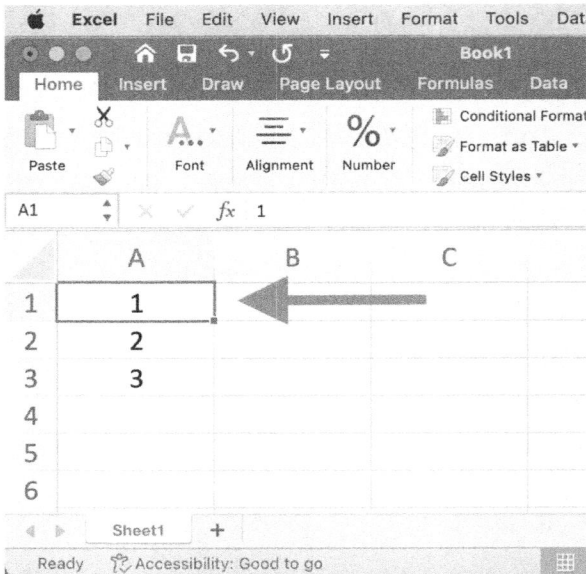

Select "Data" from the ribbon tabs.

In the Sort & Filter group, select "Sort A to Z" (ascending order) or "Sort Z to A" (descending order).

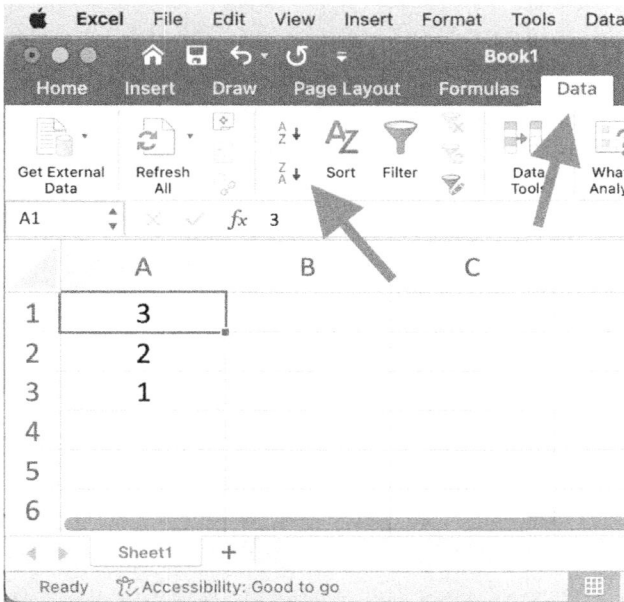

6.1.2 Sorting Using Multiple Columns

Choose any cell within the desired data range.

Select "Data" from the ribbon tabs.

In the Sort & Filter group, select the "Sort" button.

EXCEL ESSENTIALS 2023

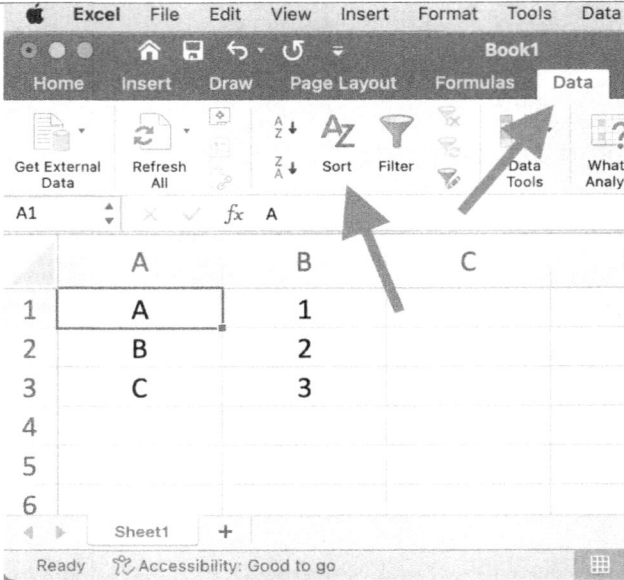

Select the principal column you wish to use for sorting in the "Sort" dialog box from the "Sort by" dropdown option. Choose whether you want the items sorted from A to Z or Z to A.

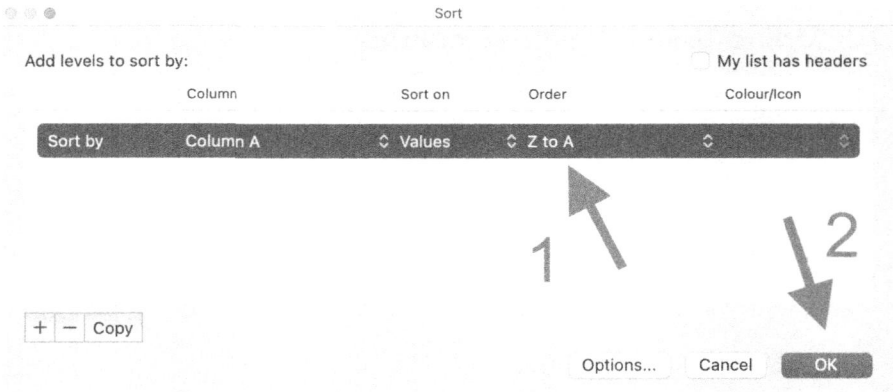

Click "OK" to apply the sort.

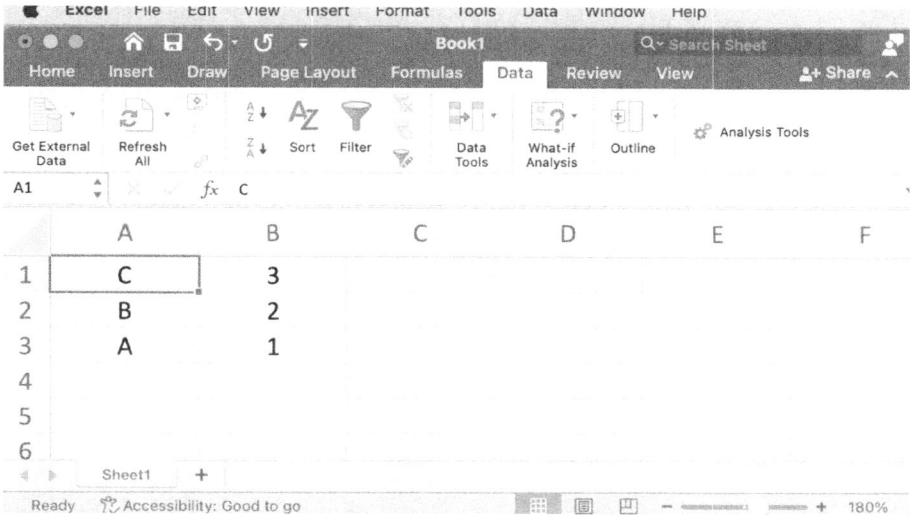

6.2 Using Filters to Show Particular Data

Filters make it simpler to concentrate on pertinent information by allowing you to see just the material that satisfies particular criteria. To apply filters to your data, follow these steps:

Choose any cell within the desired data range.

Select "Data" from the ribbon tabs.

In the Sort & Filter group, select the "Filter" button. The header row of your data will now include filter dropdown arrows.

EXCEL ESSENTIALS 2023

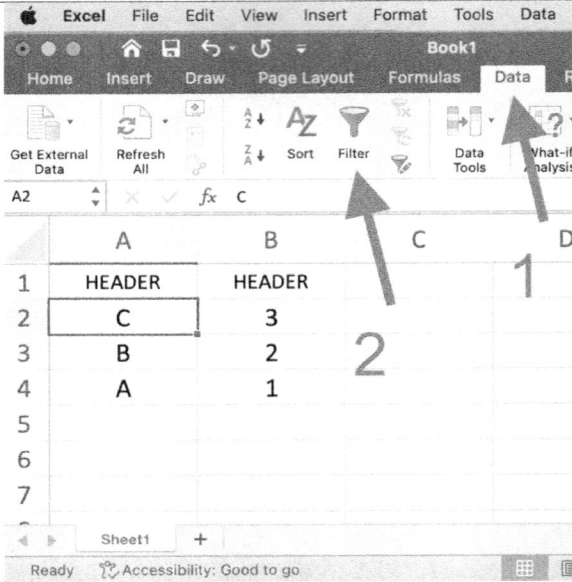

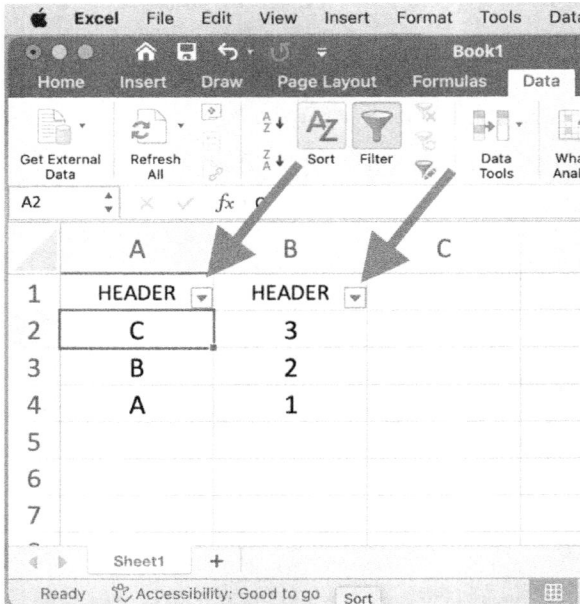

EXCEL ESSENTIALS 2023

Choose the criteria by which you wish to filter the data by clicking the filter arrow in the desired column. You may use choices like "Equals," "Greater Than," or "Contains" to filter by text, numbers, or dates.

HEADER

Sort

| A→Z ↓ Ascending | Z→A ↓ Descending |

By colour: None   ⇕

Filter

By colour: None   ⇕

✓ Choose One

Equals
Does Not Equal

Begins with
Does Not Begin with
Ends with
Does Not End with

Contains
Does Not Contain

Apply Filter   Clear Filter

To apply the filter, click "OK".

When a filter has to be cleared, click the filter arrow in the column and select "Clear Filter."

Sort

| A↓ Ascending | Z↓ Descending |

By colour: None   ⬍

Filter

By colour: None   ⬍

| Equals   ⬍ | 1 ▾ |

◉ And   ◯ Or

| Choose One   ⬍ | ▾ |

🔍 Search

☐ (Select All)
☐ 2
☐ 3
☐ 4
☐ 5

☐ Auto Apply

Apply Filter   Clear Filter

6.3 Eliminating Duplications

Duplicate data might cause your spreadsheet to be inaccurate and inconsistent. A built-in function of Excel allows you to eliminate redundant rows depending on predefined criteria. This is how to eliminate duplicate data from your system:

Choose any cell in the data range where duplicates should be eliminated.

Select "Data" from the ribbon tabs.

Select "Remove Duplicates" from the Data Tools group's menu.

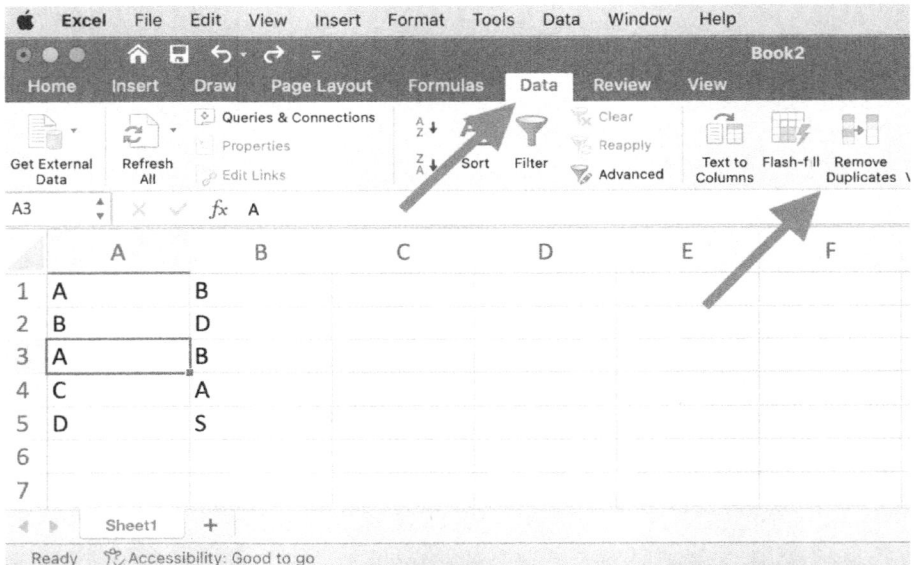

Check the boxes next to the columns you wish to use as criteria for spotting duplicates in the "Remove Duplicates" dialog box. Check the boxes next to both columns, for instance, if you wish to delete rows with identical values in columns A and B.

To get rid of duplicates, click "OK".

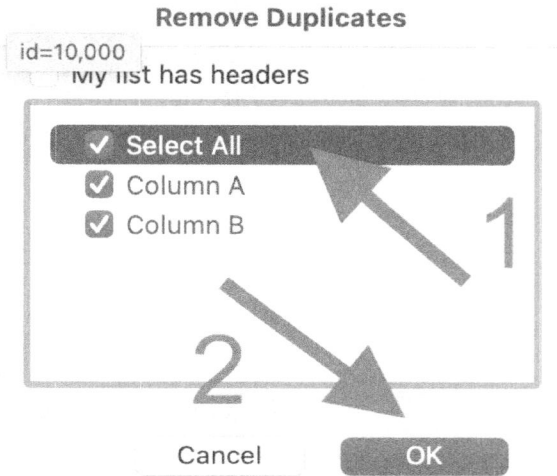

Remove Duplicates

id=10,000

My list has headers

- ✓ Select All
- ✓ Column A
- ✓ Column B

1

2

Cancel   OK

An alert from Excel will show how many duplicate rows have been eliminated and how many unique rows are still there.

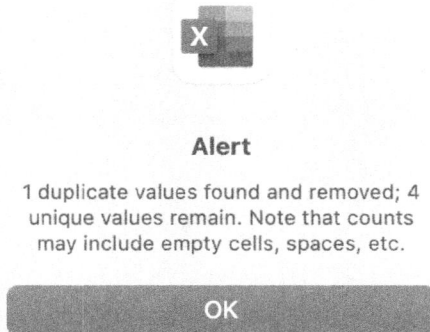

X

Alert

1 duplicate values found and removed; 4 unique values remain. Note that counts may include empty cells, spaces, etc.

OK

EXCEL ESSENTIALS 2023

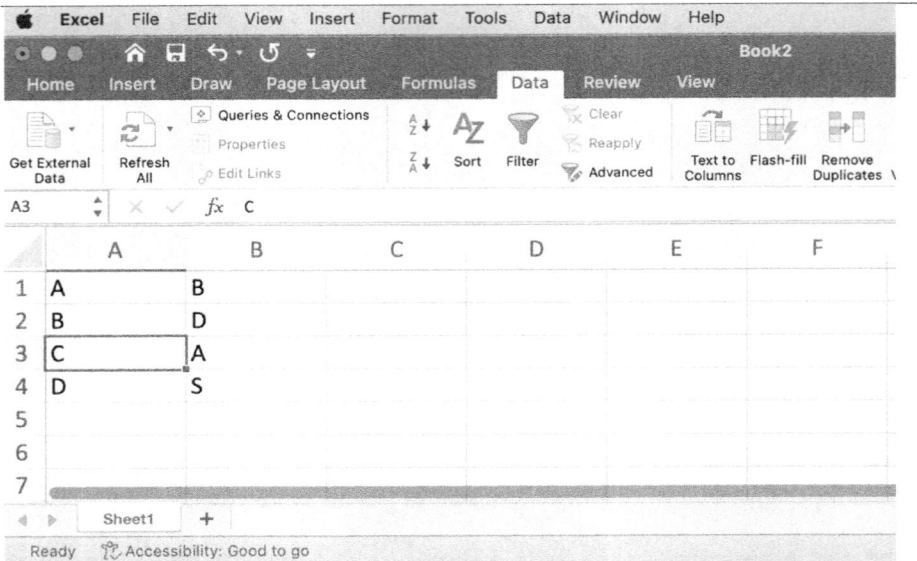

Excel's sorting, filtering, and duplication removal features will help you quickly arrange and analyze your data. The following chapters will teach you how to make charts and graphs, set up your spreadsheet for printing, and make the most of Excel.

Chapter 7: Data Visualization with Charts and Graphs

Helping you visualize your data, charts, and graphs makes it simpler to spot trends, patterns, and linkages. Each chart type available in Excel is appropriate for a certain sort of data.

7.1 Type of Graphs

Here are a few popular chart types and their applications:

Display comparisons between categories or historical trends using column and bar charts.

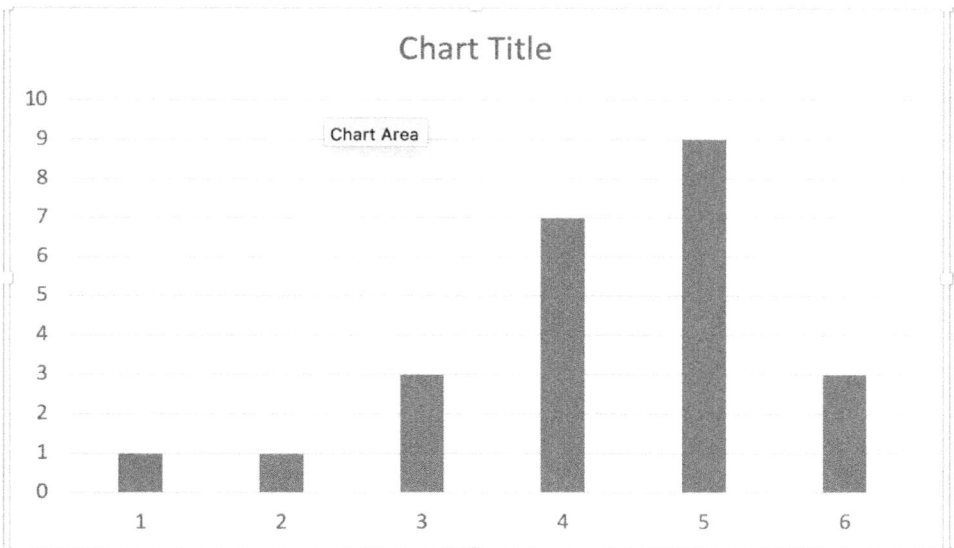

Chart Title

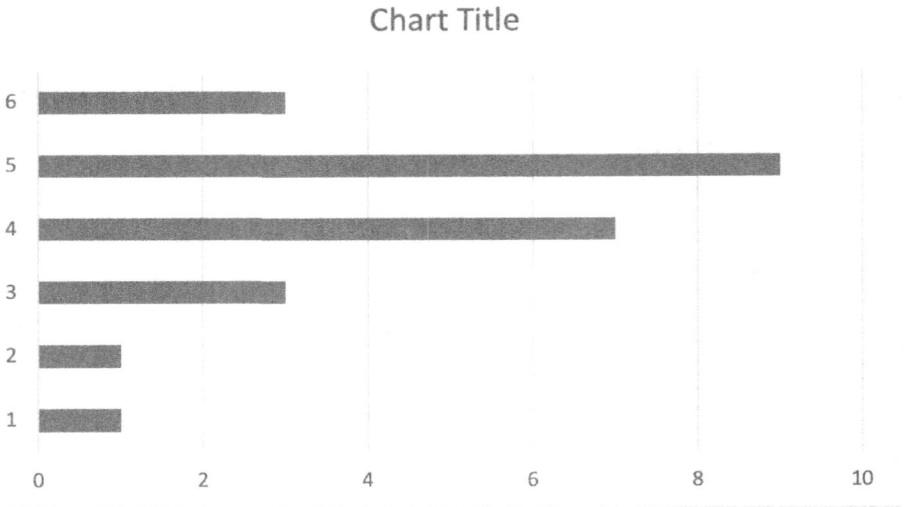

Show trends over time or continuous data with line charts.

Chart Title

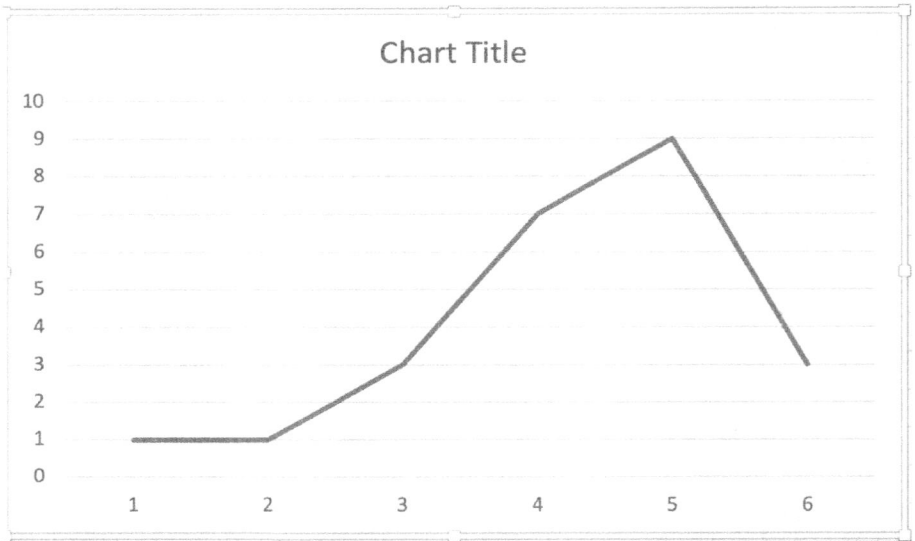

Pie charts: Show percentages or proportions of a whole.

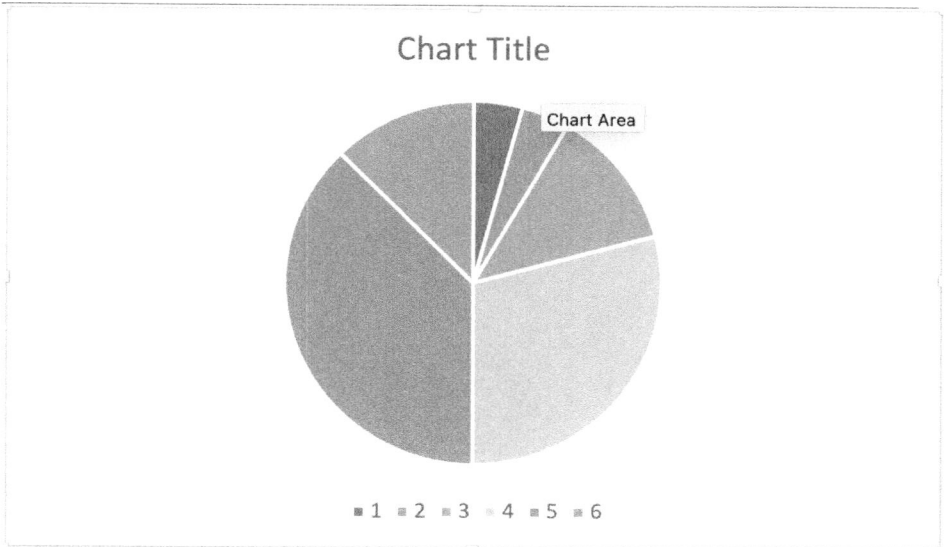

Display correlations between two sets of data using scatter plots.

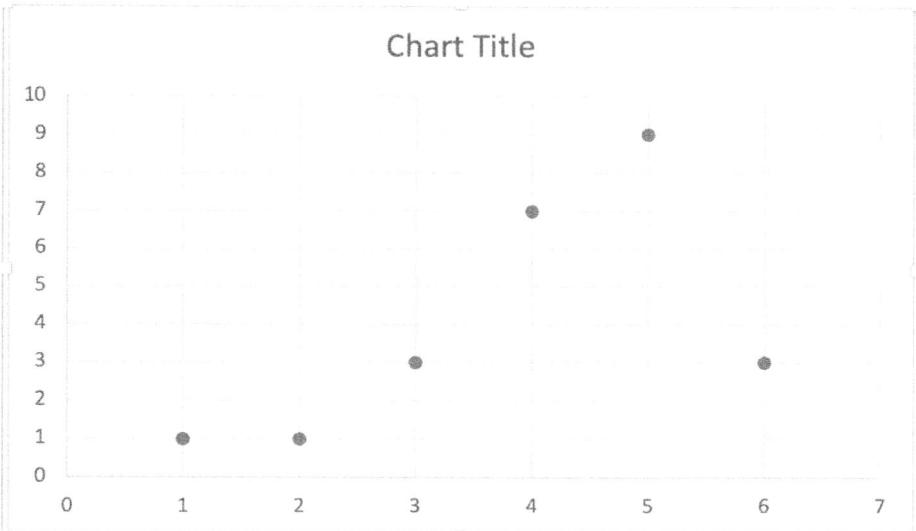

Area charts: Highlight magnitude while displaying trends over time.

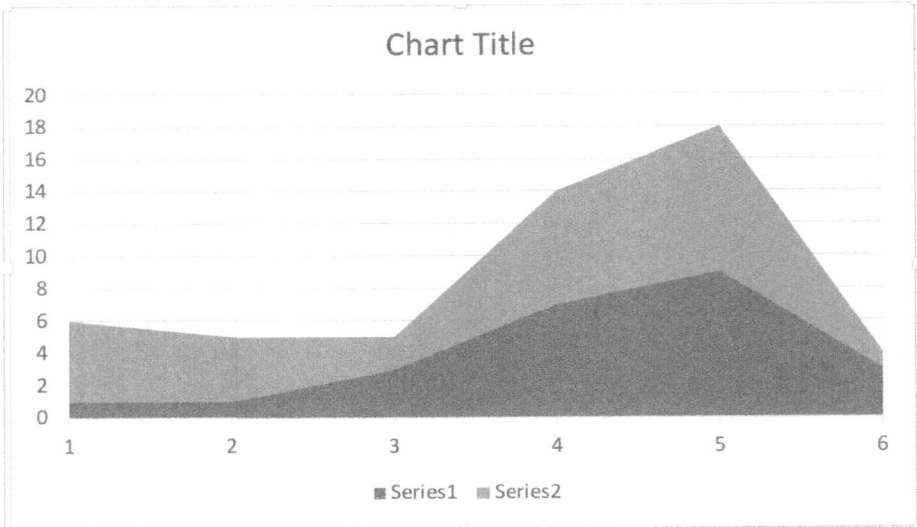

Select a chart type that effectively communicates your ideas and best reflects your data.

7.2 Chart Design

These instructions will help you build a chart in Excel after you've selected the appropriate chart type:

Choose the data range that will be shown in the graphic.

The "Insert" tab will be selected in the ribbon.

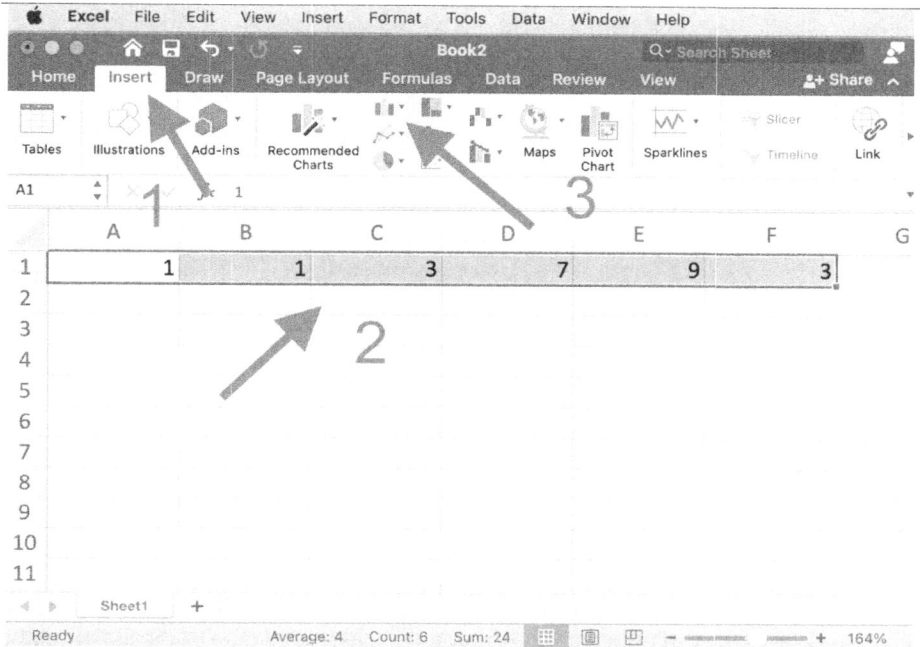

From the Charts group, select the required chart type. For instance, choose a 2D or 3D column chart by clicking the "Column" option.

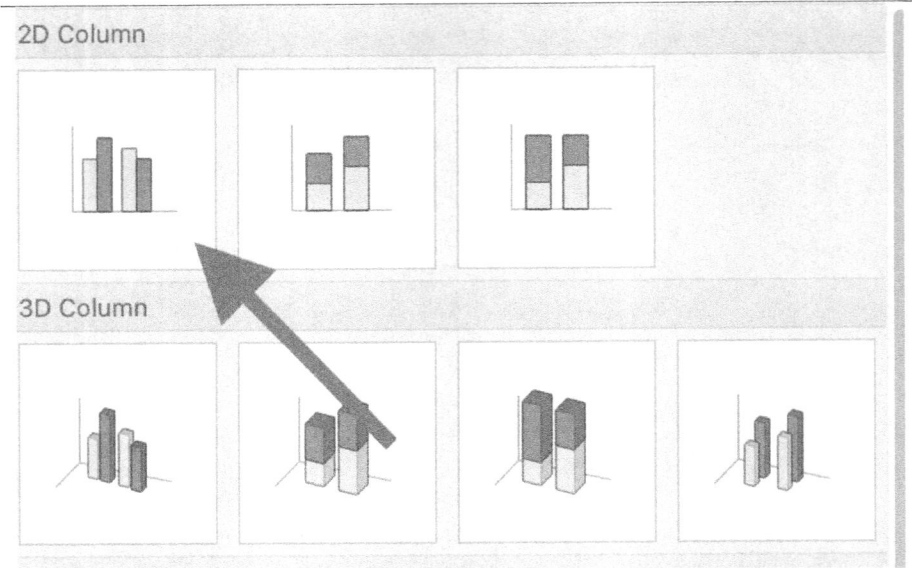

Excel will add the chart to your spreadsheet, graphically presenting your data.

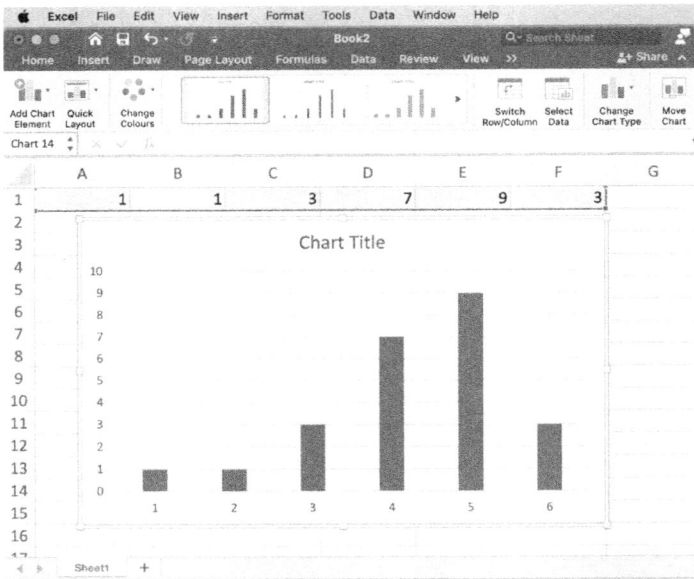

7.3 Making Your Chart Your Own

Excel offers many customization options to help you create a chart that suits your taste. How to modify your chart is as follows:

7.3.1 Resizing and repositioning the chart

To resize a chart, click and drag one of the scaling handles (small circles) at the chart's border after clicking the chart to select it.

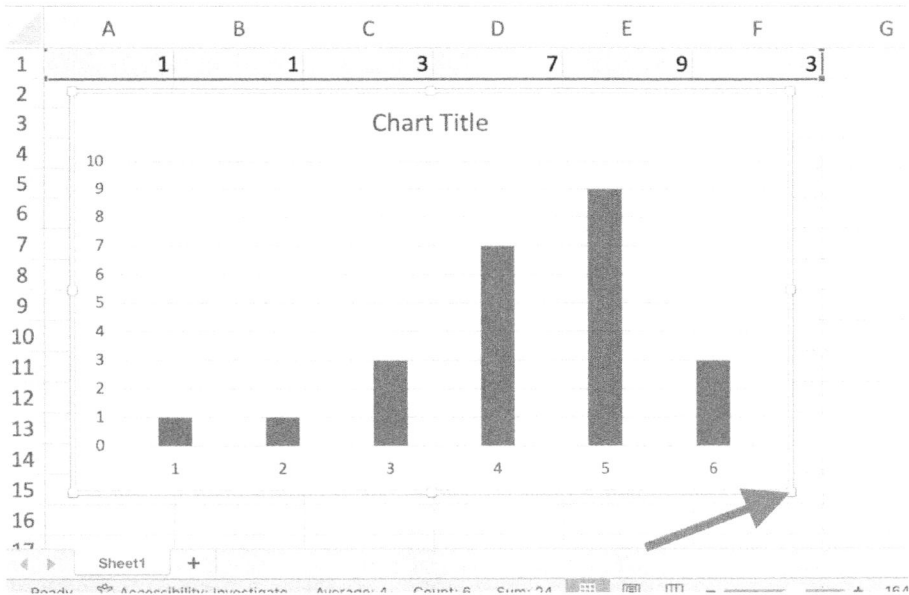

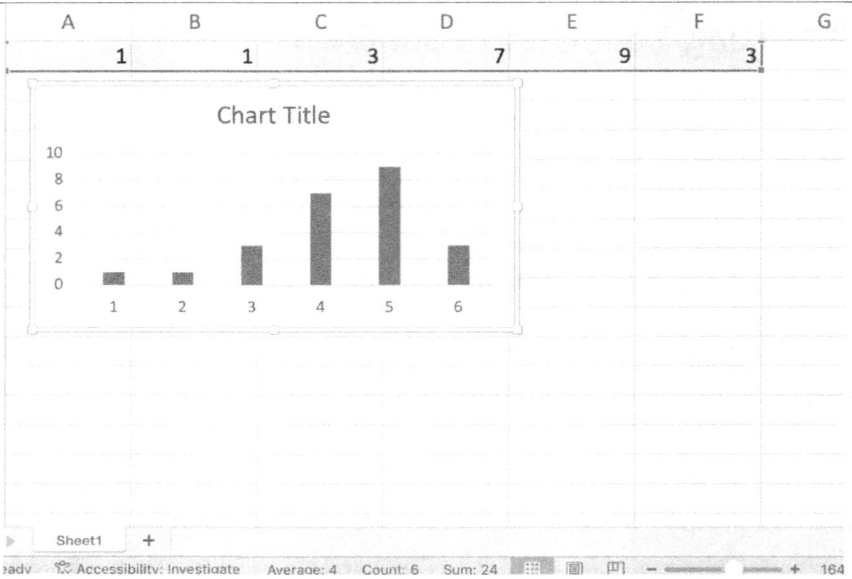

To reposition a chart within a worksheet, click it to select it, then click and drag the chart's border.

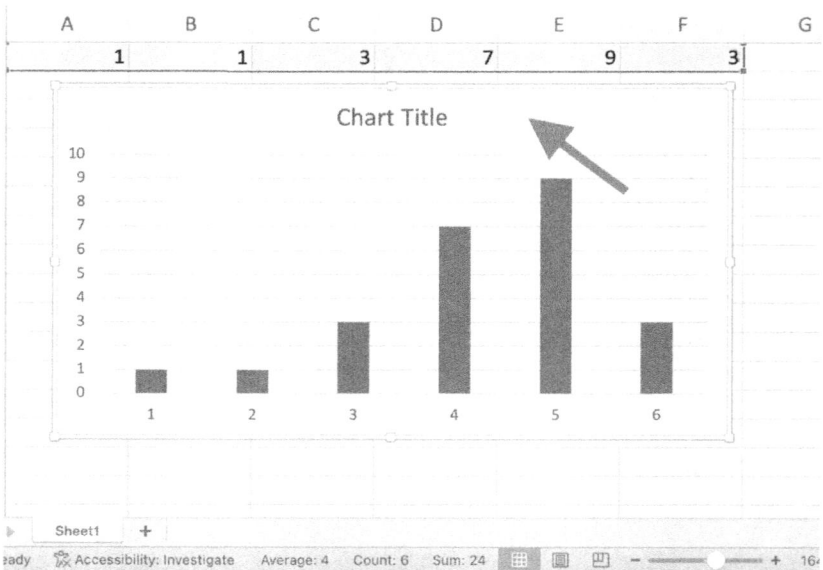

7.3.2 Formatting Chart Elements

Use the following steps to format certain chart components, such as the title, axis labels, or data series:

To choose a chart, click on it.

To format a chart element, such as the title of the chart or a data series, simply click on it.

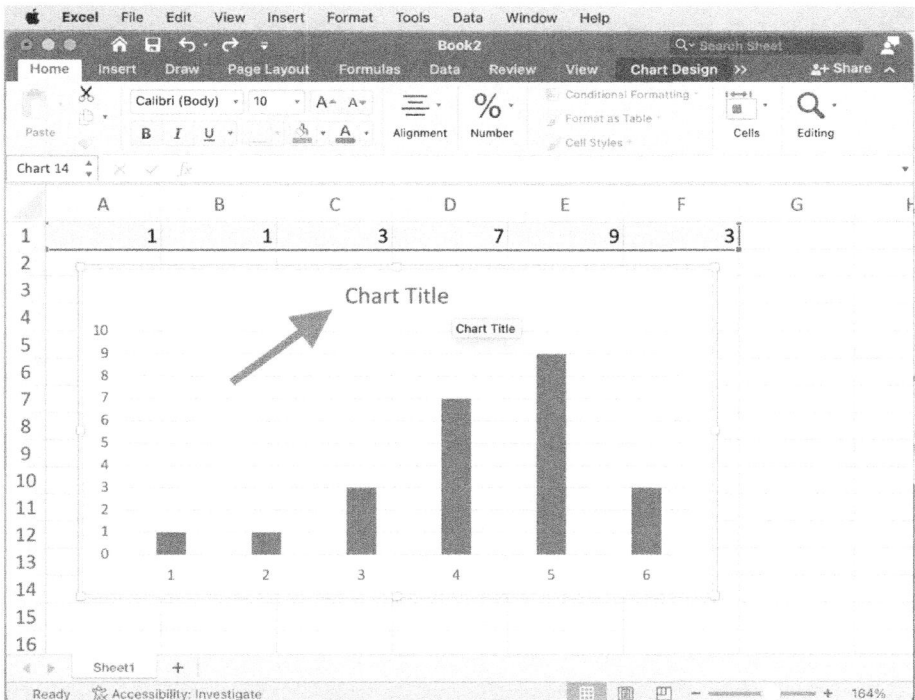

To format an element, right-click on it and pick "Format [element]" from the context menu (for example, "Format Chart Title").

Delete

Reset to Match Style

Edit Text

Font...

Change Chart Type   >

Select Data...

3D Rotation...

Format Chart Title...

Services   >

Delete

Reset to Match Style

Edit Text

Font...

Change Chart Type   >

Select Data...

3D Rotation...

Format Chart Title...

Services   >

Use the Font, Color, and Style choices to alter the element's look in the display Format window.

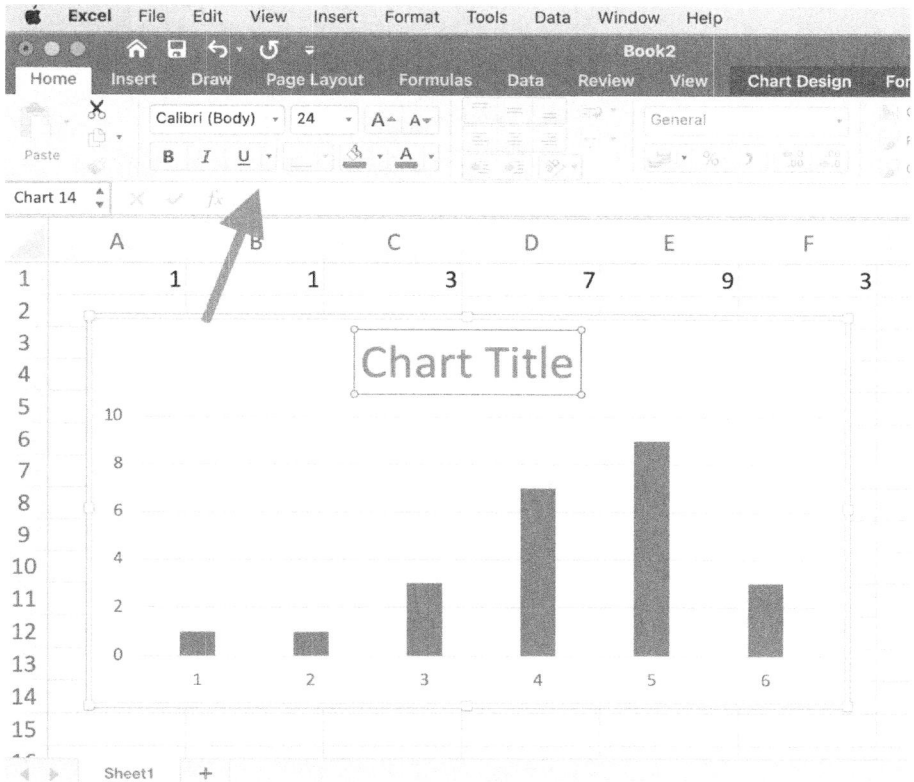

7.3.3 Changes to the Chart Style

Excel has many pre-built chart styles that let you rapidly alter the appearance of your chart. Observe these procedures to alter the chart's style:

To choose a chart, click on it.

The "Chart Design" tab will appear in the ribbon.

You may select a certain chart style by clicking on the chosen thumbnail in the Chart Styles group.

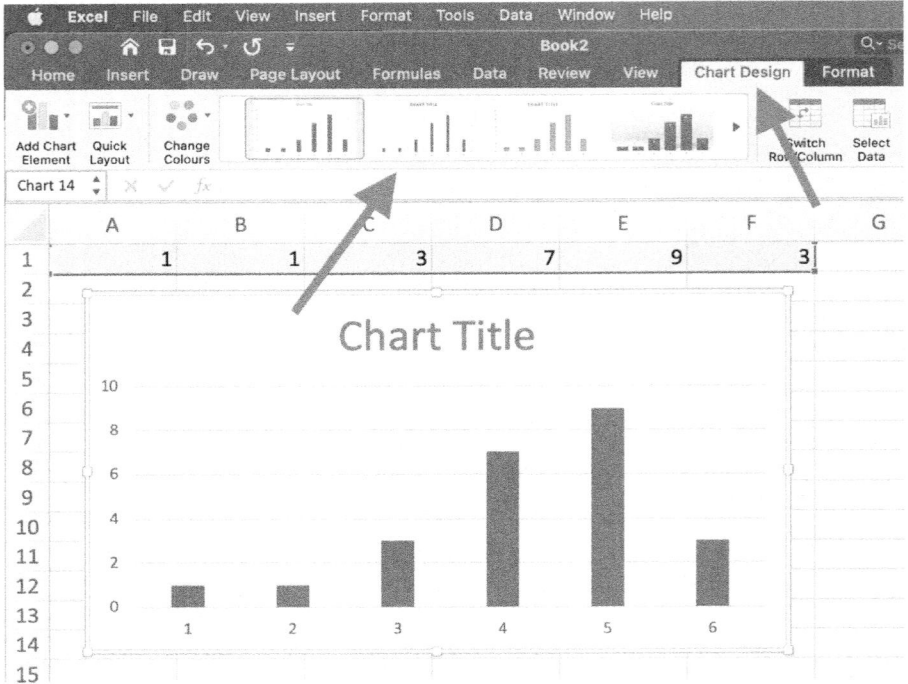

7.4 Modifying and Editing Data for Charts

You might need to modify your chart as you update or alter your data. To update and alter chart data, follow these steps:

7.4.1 Update Chart Data

You may quickly update your chart to reflect this data if you add new data to your worksheet:

To choose a chart, click on it.

The "Chart Design" tab will appear in the ribbon.

In the Data group, select the "Select Data" button.

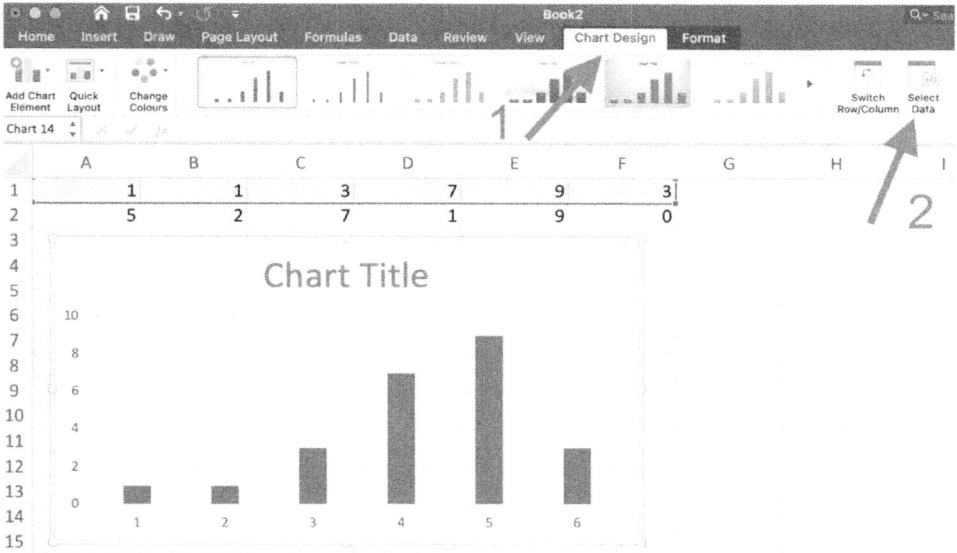

Change the data range in the "Select Data Source" dialog box to incorporate the new data, then click "OK."

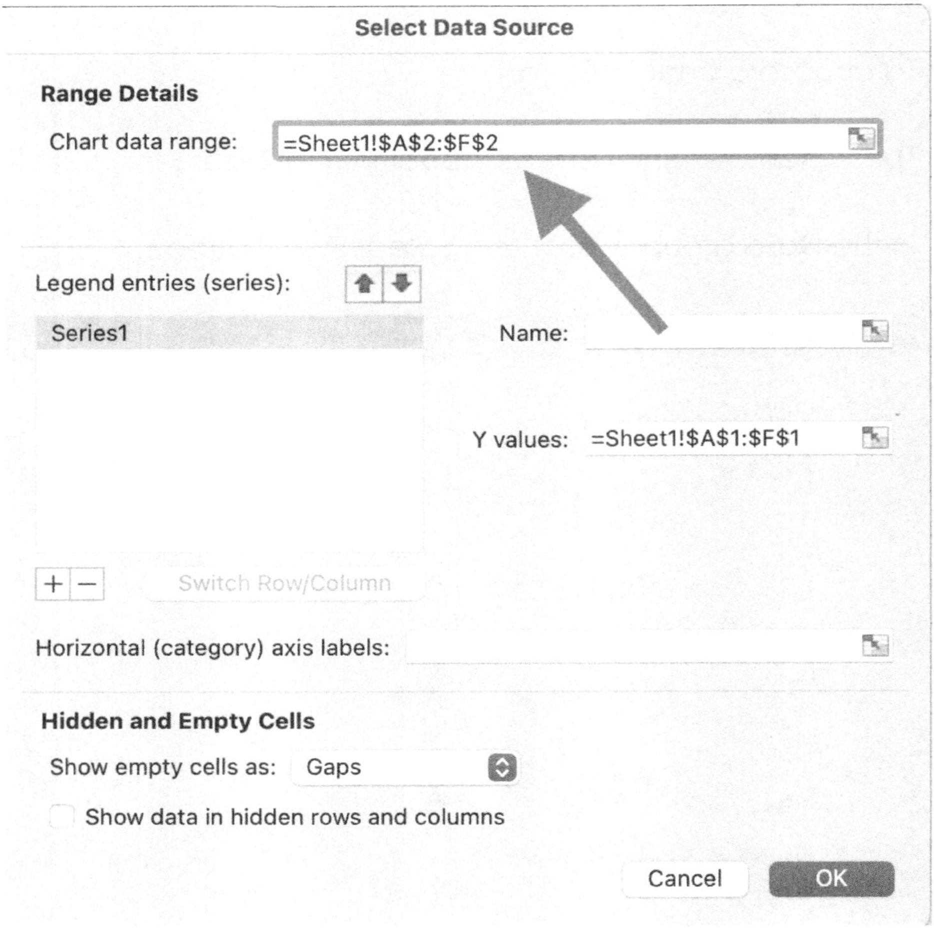

EXCEL ESSENTIALS 2023

Select Data Source

Range Details

Chart data range: | =Sheet1!$A$2:$F$2

Legend entries (series): ⬆ ⬇

Series1   Name:

Y values: =Sheet1!$A$1:$F$1

| + | − | Switch Row/Column

Horizontal (category) axis labels:

Hidden and Empty Cells

Show empty cells as: Gaps ⬍

☐ Show data in hidden rows and columns

Cancel   OK

The new data range will now be reflected in your chart.

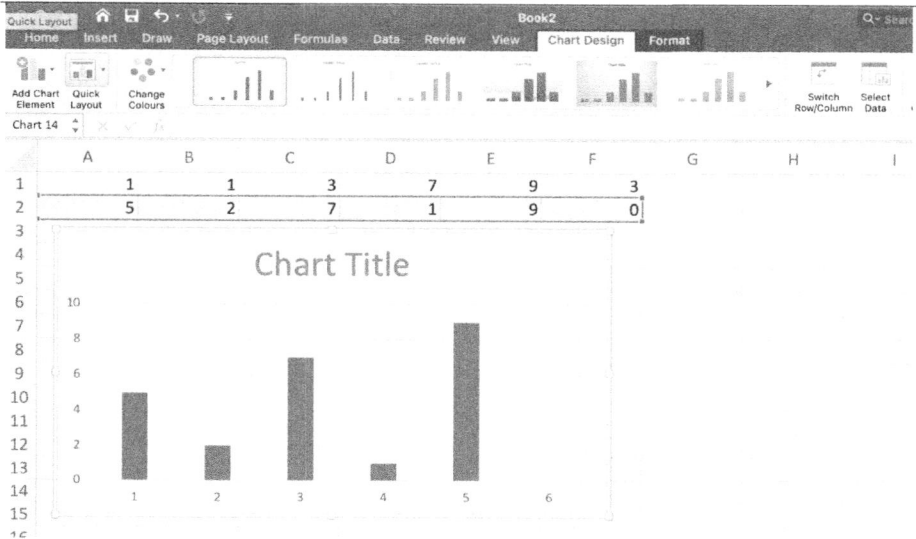

7.4.2 Editing Data Series and Categories

The procedures below can be used to change the data series or categories in your chart.

To choose a chart, click on it.

The "Chart Design" tab will appear in the Ribbon.

In the Data group, select the "Select Data" button.

EXCEL ESSENTIALS 2023

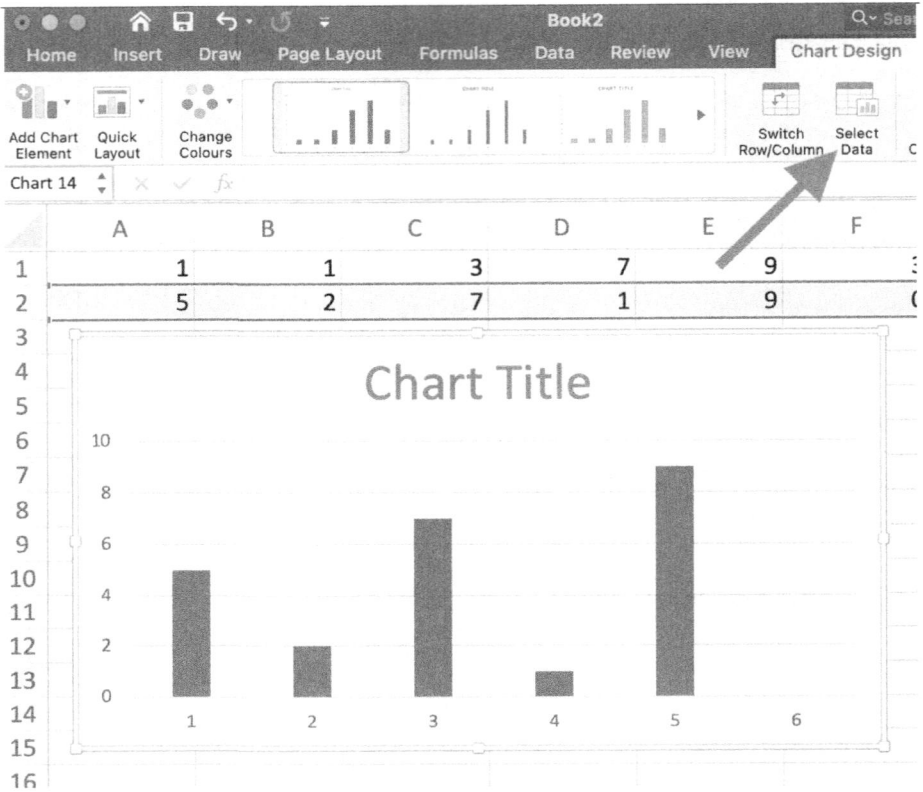

You may update data series and categories by adding, deleting, or changing the items in the "Legend Entries (Series)" and "Horizontal (Category) Axis Labels" lists in the "Select Data Source" dialog box.

Select Data Source

Range Details

Chart data range: =Sheet1!$A$2:$F$2

1

Legend entries (series): ⬆ ⬇

Series1   Name:

                          Y values: =Sheet1!$A$2:$F$2

                                                    2

+ −   Switch Row/Column

Horizontal (category) axis labels:

Hidden and Empty Cells

Show empty cells as: Gaps

3

☐ Show data in hidden rows and columns

                              Cancel   OK

You may efficiently display and convey your data insights by generating and modifying charts and graphs in Excel. The following chapter will teach you how to prepare your spreadsheet for printing and provide you with Excel use advice.

Chapter 8: Tips and Preparing Your Spreadsheet for Printing

8.1 Making the Print Area

You must set the print area before printing your spreadsheet to guarantee that just the appropriate data is printed. How to set the print area is as follows:

Choose the range of cells you wish the print area to contain.

In the Ribbon, select the "Page Layout" tab.

In the Page Setup group, click the "Print Area" button.

EXCEL ESSENTIALS 2023

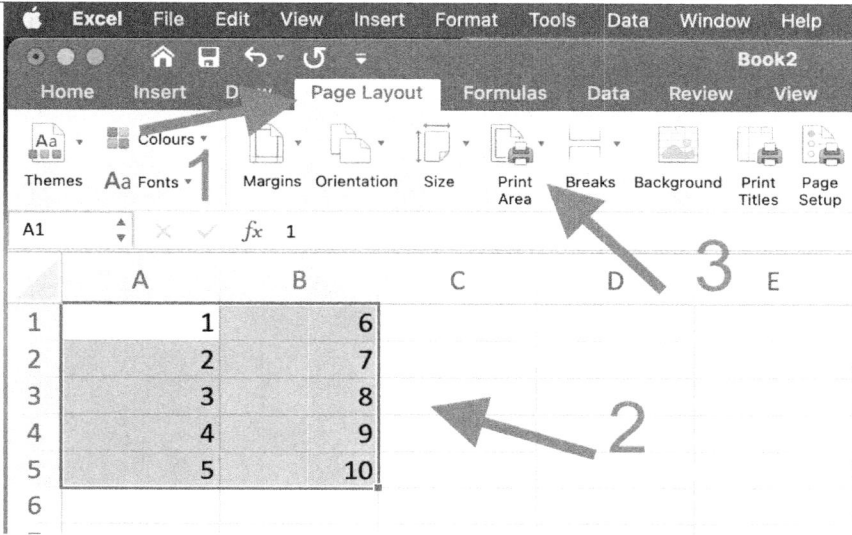

From the dropdown menu, select "Set Print Area".

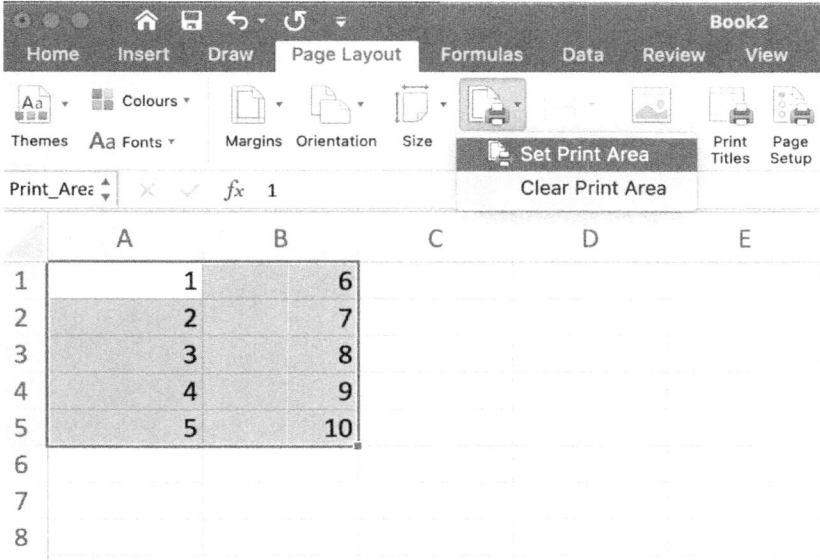

Click the "Print Area" button and select "Clear Print Area" to clear the print area.

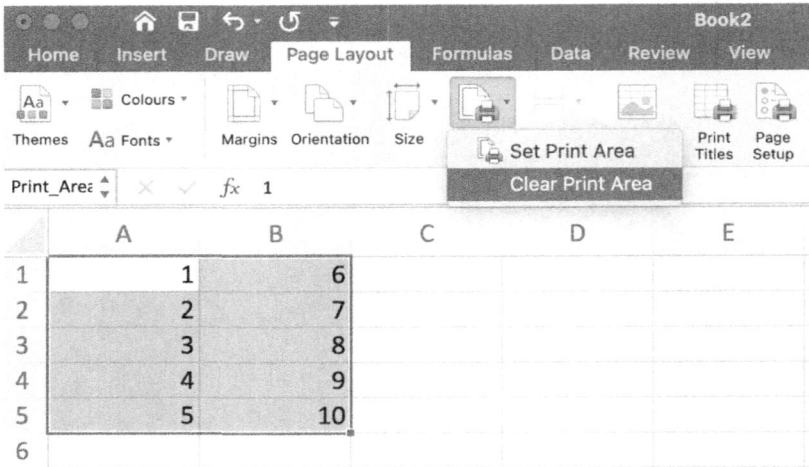

Adjusting the scaling and page layout

Your printed spreadsheet can look better if the page layout and scale are changed. How to change these parameters is as follows:

8.2 Altering Page Size and Orientation

In the Ribbon, select the "Page Layout" tab.

Click the "Orientation" button in the Page Setup group and select "Portrait" or "Landscape" from the dropdown menu.

EXCEL ESSENTIALS 2023

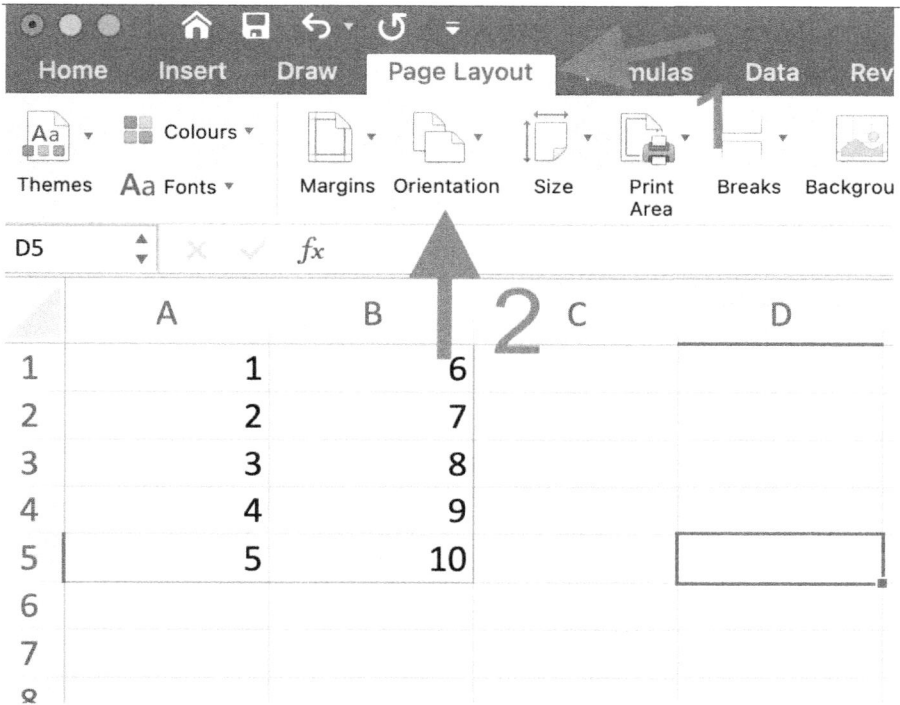

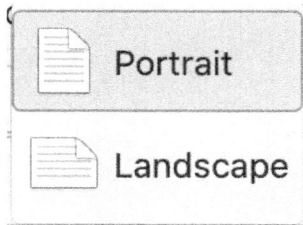

Click the "Size" button and choose the desired choice from the drop-down menu to alter the paper size.

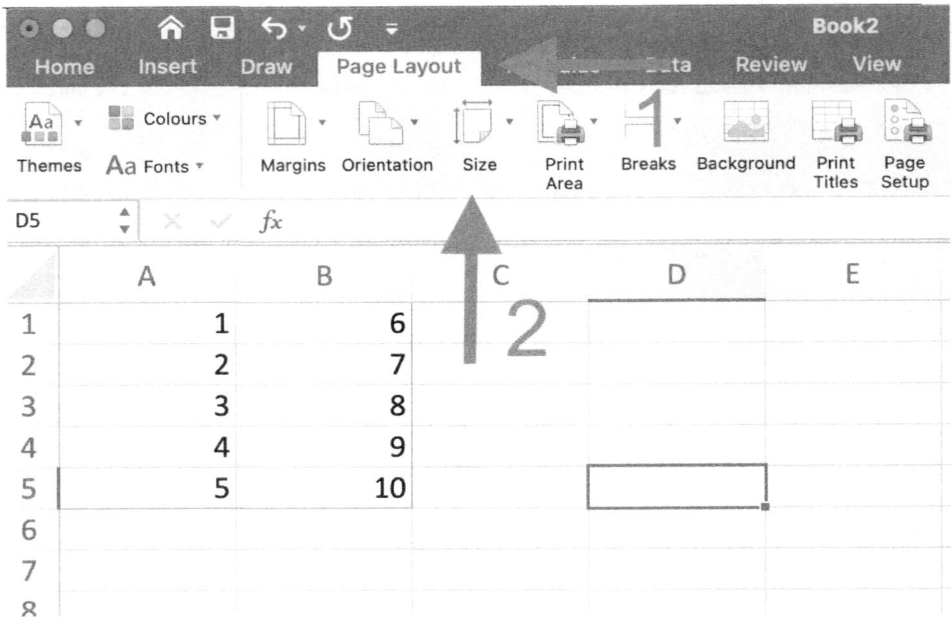
Book2
Home
Insert
Draw
Page Layout
Review
View
1
Themes
Colours
Aa Fonts
Margins
Orientation
Size
Print Area
Breaks
Background
Print Titles
Page Setup
D5
fx
A
B
C
D
E
2
1 1 6
2 2 7
3 3 8
4 4 9
5 5 10
6
7

Letter 8½ x 11 in
8,5" x 11"

Letter Small 8½ x 11 in
8,5" x 11"

Tabloid 11 x 17 in
11" x 17"

Ledger 17 x 11 in
17" x 11"

Legal 8½ x 14 in
8,5" x 14"

Statement 5½ x 8½ in
5,5" x 8,5"

Executive 7½ x 10 in
7,25" x 10,5"

A3 297 x 420 mm
11,69" x 16,54"

A4 210 x 297 mm
8,26" x 11,69"

A4 Small 210 x 297 mm
8,26" x 11,69"

A5 148 x 210 mm
5,83" x 8,26"

A6 105 x 148 mm
4,14" x 5,83"

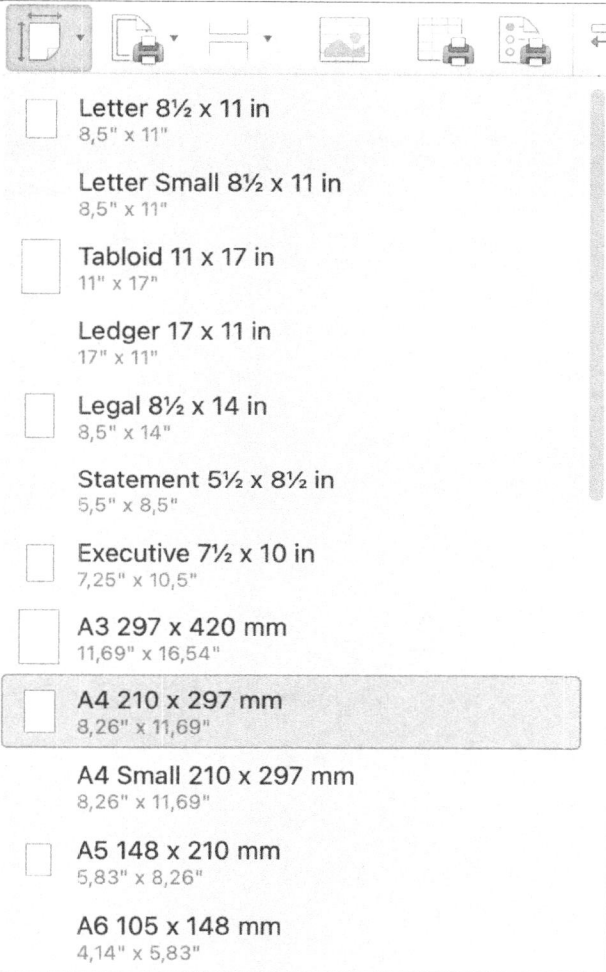

Scaling Your Spreadsheet for the Page 8.2.2

In the Ribbon, select the "Page Layout" tab.

Use the "Width" and "Height" drop-down choices in the Scale to Fit group to change the scaling. Select a particular number of pages or "Automatic" to let Excel choose the optimum match.

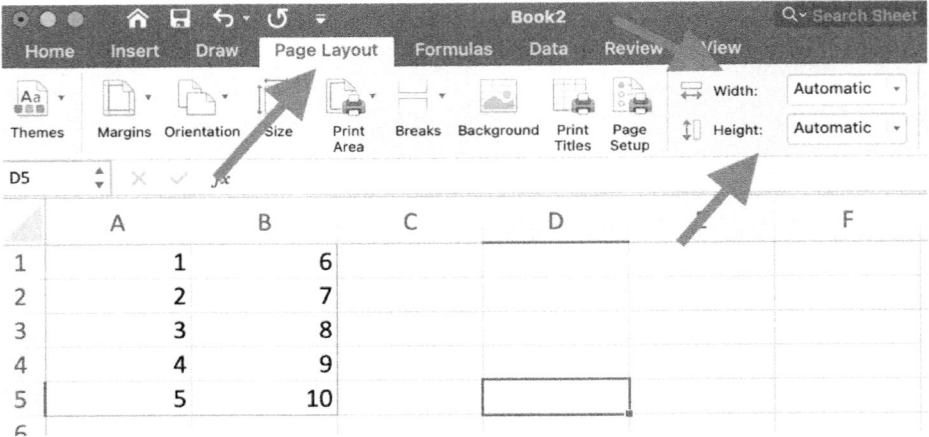

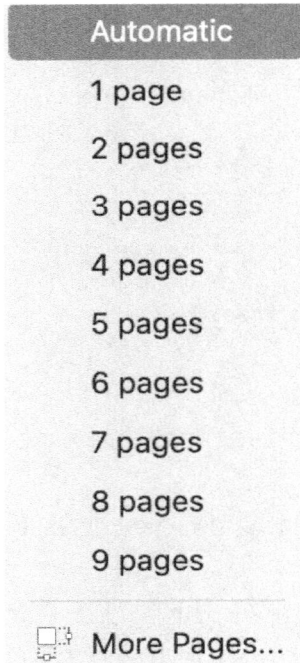

8.3 Addition of Headers and Footers

The printed spreadsheet's headers and footers might show extra details like page numbers, dates, or logos. To add headers and footers, follow these steps:

The "Insert" tab will be selected in the ribbon.

Select "Header & Footer" under the Text category.

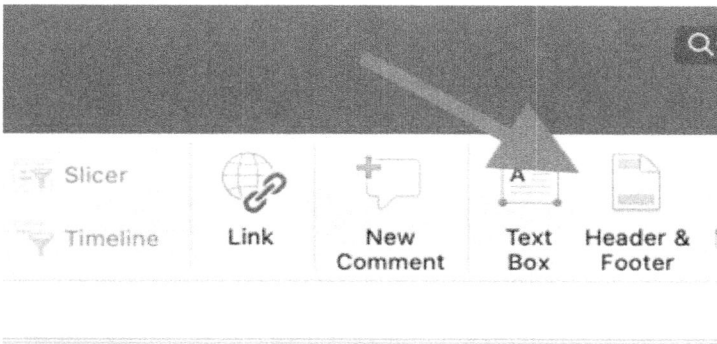

The display will change to Page Layout in Excel. To modify the content, click on the header or footer section.

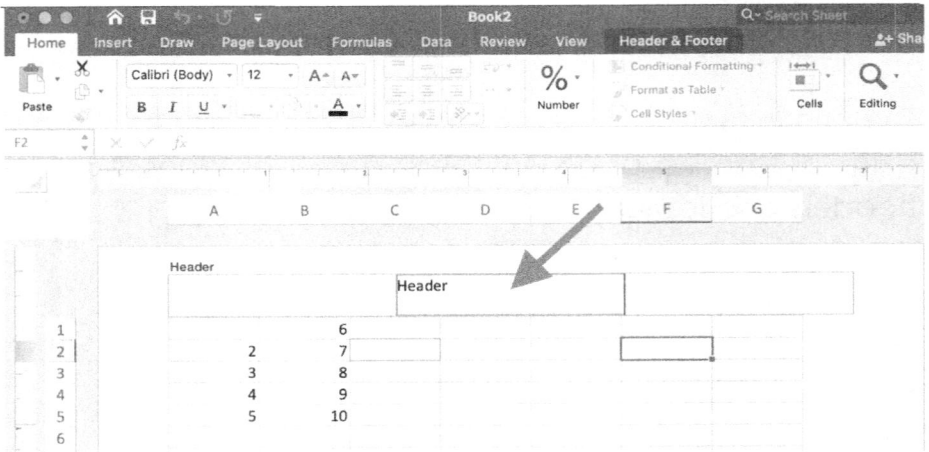

To add components like page numbers, dates, or photos, use Ribbon's Header & Footer Tools Design tab.

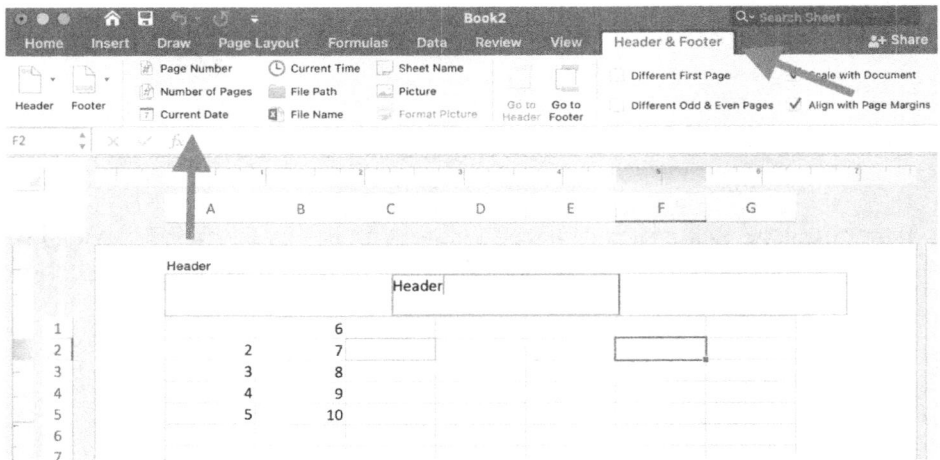

8.4 Checking Your Spreadsheet Out and Printing It

It's a good idea to preview your spreadsheet before printing to make sure everything looks as you intend. To preview and print your spreadsheet, follow these steps:

In the Ribbon, choose the "File" tab and then choose "Print."

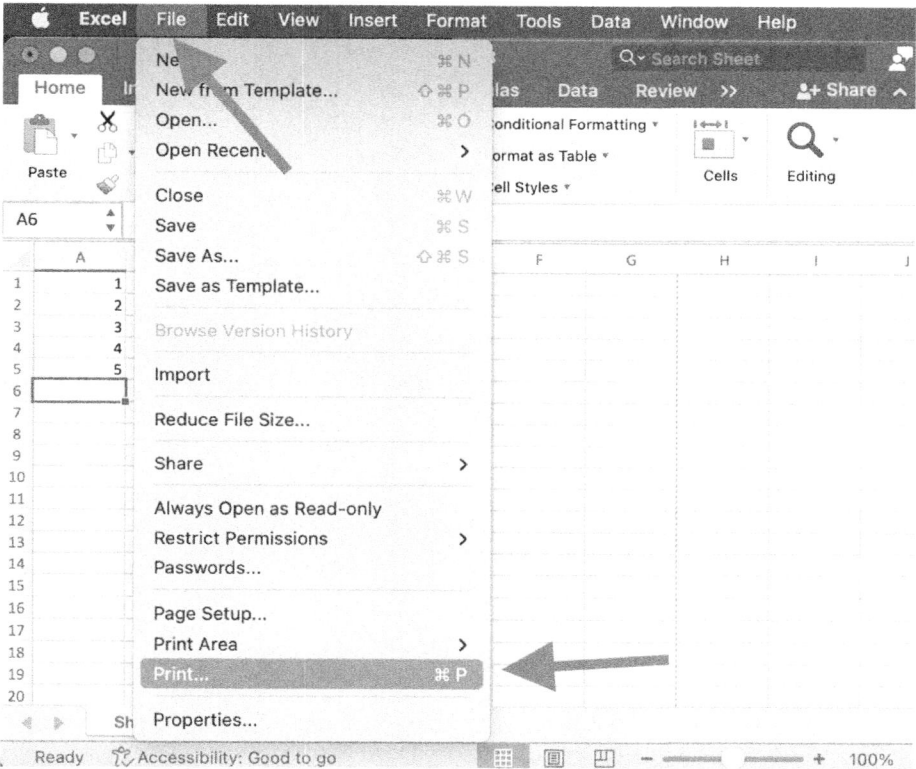

You may get a preview of your spreadsheet in the Print pane. Examine the preview and change any print settings that need to be changed, such as selecting a printer, stating the number of copies, or modifying the page layout.

To print your spreadsheet, click the Print button.

EXCEL ESSENTIALS 2023

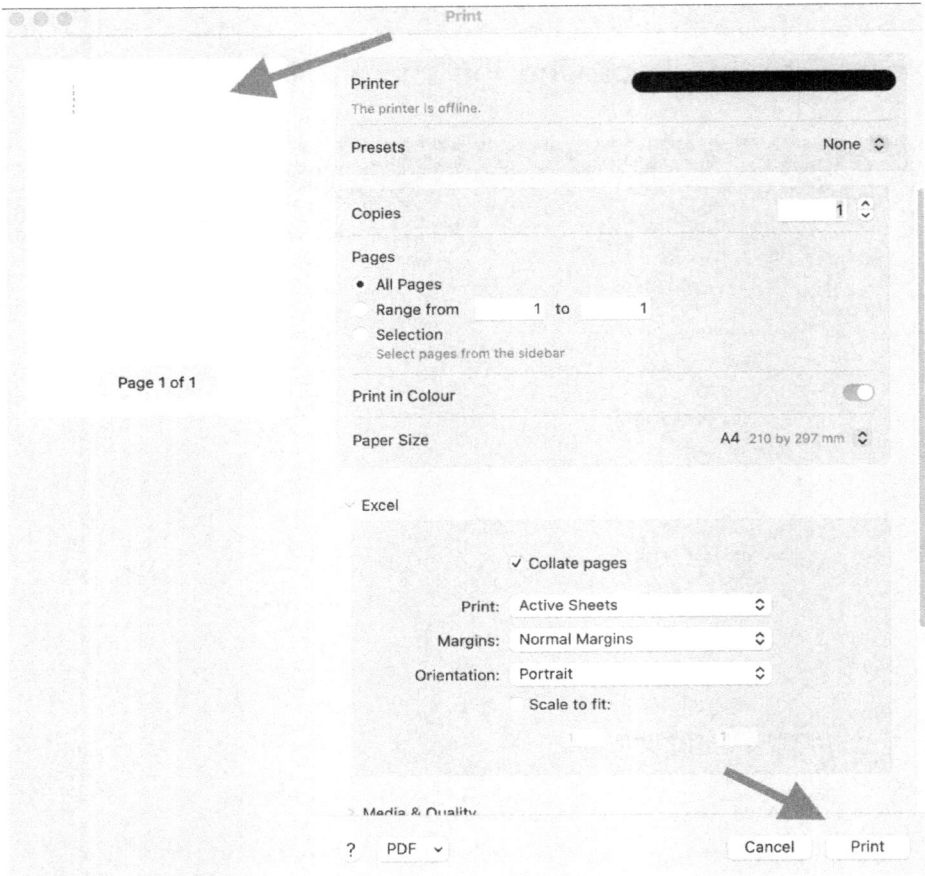

You're prepared to distribute your work to others after your spreadsheet is set up for printing. We'll look at some advice for maximizing Excel in this last segment.

Chapter 9: Advice for Excel Newcomers

9.1 Keyboard shortcuts

Excel keyboard shortcuts may speed up and simplify your process. Following are some typical Excel shortcuts:

Command + C: Copy

Paste with Ctrl + V

Shift + X to cut

Undo with Ctrl + Z

Shift + Y: Undo

Ctrl + F to search

Replace with Ctrl + H

Save with Ctrl + S

Open with Ctrl + O

Print with Ctrl + P.

Learn how to use these shortcuts to increase your Excel productivity.

9.2 Actions You Can Undo and Repeat

Excel can undo, redo, and repeat operations so that you may fix errors or use the same action on numerous cells at once. How to use these functionalities is as follows:

Press Ctrl + Z or click the "Undo" icon on the Quick Access Toolbar to reverse your most recent action.

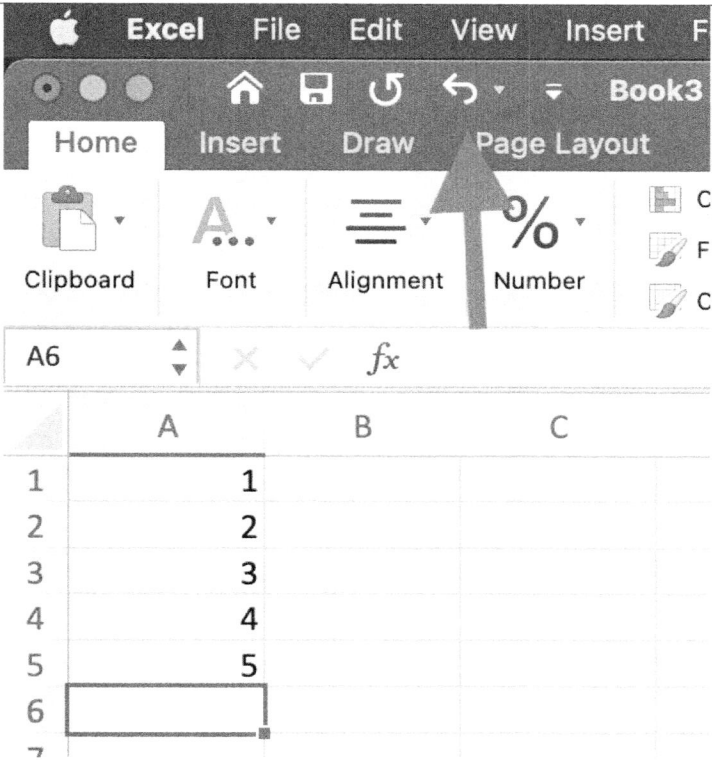

Press Ctrl + Y, F4, or the "Repeat" button on the Quick Access Toolbar (if present) to redo your last operation.

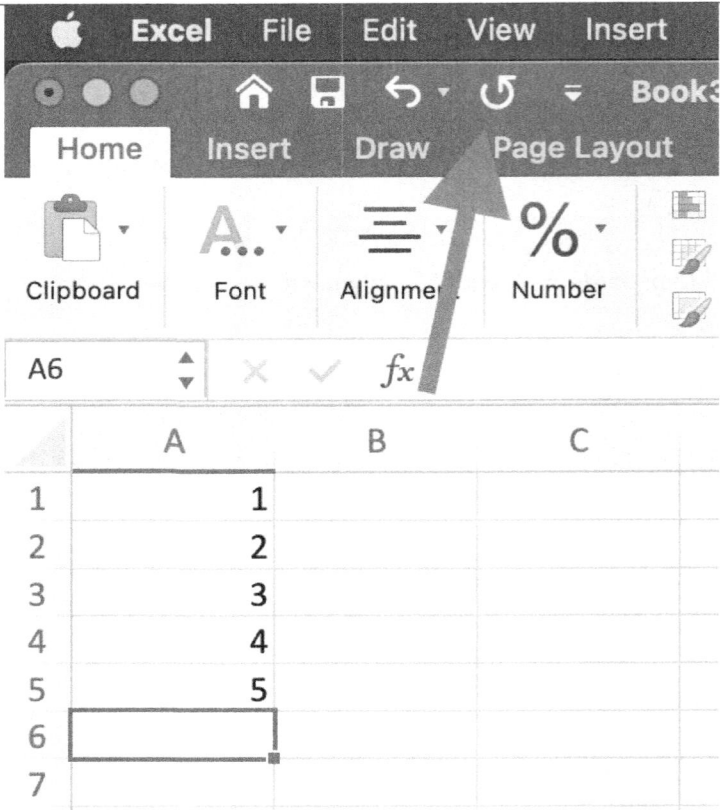

These tools can make your job more productive and speed up error correction.

9.3 Utilizing the Help Function

You may use the built-in help function in Excel to obtain answers to your queries and discover more information about particular functions and features. Here's how to get support with Excel:

EXCEL ESSENTIALS 2023

Either use the F1 key on your keyboard or select the "Help" button in the Excel window's upper right corner (it looks like a question mark).

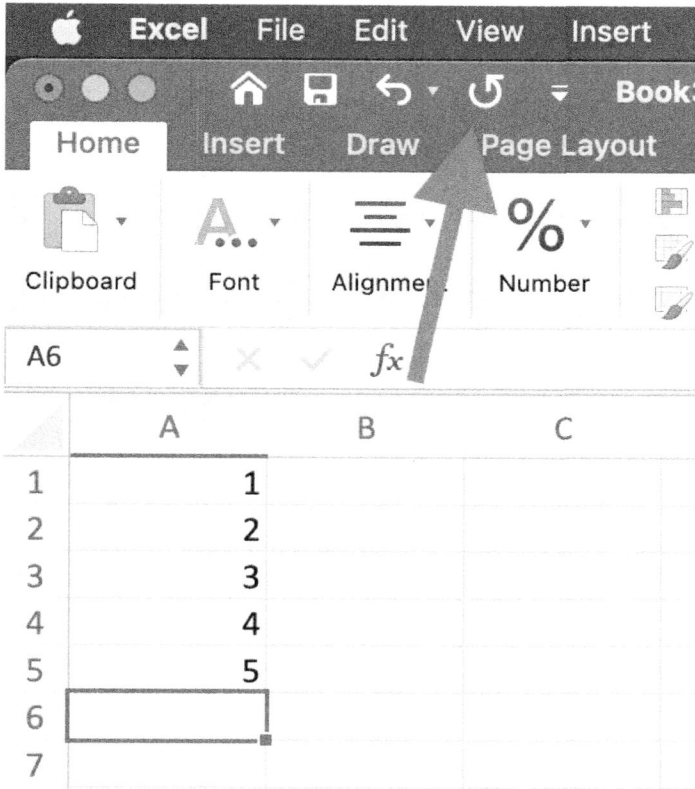

Enter a term or question associated with your search in the help window.

Review the search results to locate pertinent articles, lessons, or videos.

You may find out how to carry out certain activities or fix difficulties as they come up by utilizing Excel's help function.

9.4 Organizational Best Practices for Spreadsheets

Keeping a spreadsheet structured is essential for precise data analysis and a smooth workflow. Here are some spreadsheet organizing recommended practices:

9.4.1 Employ Definable Headers

You can better grasp the data and find particular information using clear and detailed headers for your columns and rows. Be consistent with formatting your headers, such as utilizing strong font or contrasting background colors to set them apart from the data.

9.4.2 Maintain a group of related data

Create order in your spreadsheet by grouping similar data in neighboring columns or rows. Making computations, charts, or applying filters to pertinent data is much simpler.

9.4.3 Independent Reports, Calculations, and Data

Make separate pages for the raw data, computations, and reports or summaries in your worksheet. This simplifies updating and analyzing your data by preserving a tidy and structured structure.

9.4.4 Correctly Format Cells

To guarantee consistency and enhance readability, format cells by the data type they contain (for example, currency, percentage, or date). You may format cells using the "Number" group on the Home tab in the Ribbon.

9.4.5 Utilize Cell Notes or Comments

Add comments or notes to specific cells to provide more context or information about the data. Right-click the cell and select "New Note" or "New Comment" from the context menu to add a comment or note.

By adhering to these organizing spreadsheet best practices, you'll make Excel more effective and user-friendly. Beginners must adopt solid habits and methods to serve them well as they advance their understanding of Excel.

Chapter 10: Conclusion and Next

This book has covered a variety of Excel features and functions that may be used to create spreadsheets and carry out tasks effectively in both professional and personal settings. Even though we've covered a lot of crucial subjects, Excel is capable of a lot more.

Excel is a strong tool with many uses, from straightforward data organizing to intricate financial analysis and data visualization. As you experiment and explore Excel, you'll find new strategies and features targeted to your particular requirements and sector.

The information you learned from this book will be a solid starting point for your work with Excel. You are well-equipped to handle various jobs and obstacles by gaining proficiency in the fundamentals, including data input, formatting, and basic formulas.

If you would like to explore further and become a true Excel expert, I have written a more comprehensive book that will guide you step by step through this program's advanced features, allowing you to master it even more effectively.

The complete book will give you several bonuses and free access to three exclusive video courses designed to help you better and more quickly understand the various functions of Excel.

You can always find the book EXCEL 2023 on Amazon.

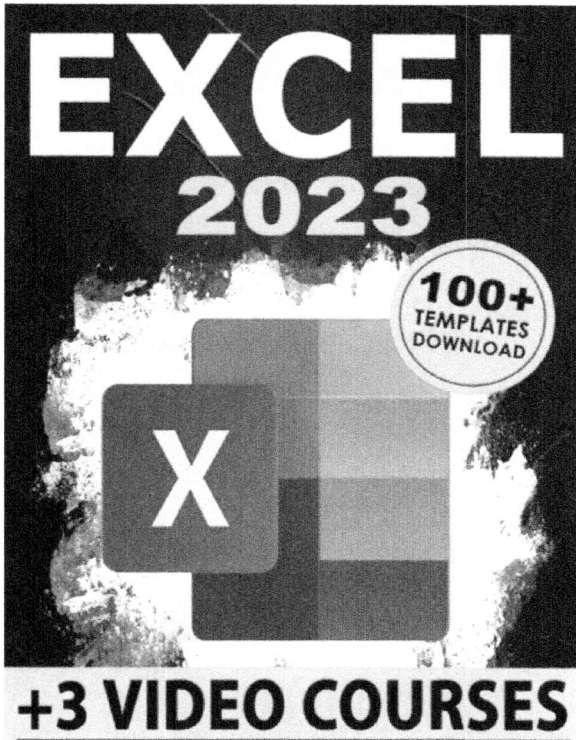

The book includes the following Bonuses:

Get Ready to Elevate Your Excel Game Like Never Before! This Isn't Just any Ordinary Book - It's a Complete Journey Course Designed to Transform You Into an EXCEL 2023 MASTER!

Whether you're just starting out or you're a seasoned pro looking to expand your skills, this book is the perfect resource. With its easy-to-follow lessons and ready-to-use templates, you'll be well on your way to becoming a top-notch data analyst. Don't miss out on this amazing opportunity to level up your career!

THIS BOOK INCLUDES

#1 - EXCEL Video Course *BEGINNER*

The video course is perfect for anyone who wants to improve their Excel skills, from students and job seekers to professionals and small business owners

#2 - EXCEL Video Course *INTERMEDIATE*

This course is perfect for anyone who wants to develop their Excel skills further, from business professionals to data analysts, financial experts, and entrepreneurs

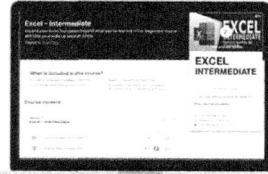

#3 - EXCEL Video Course *ADVANCED*

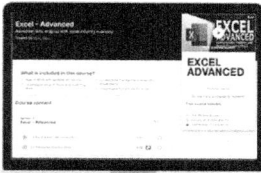

It's perfect for advanced users who want to become Excel power users, including financial analysts, data scientists, and business intelligence professionals

#4 - 100+ Ready-to-Use Templates

No more struggling to create complicated documents from scratch, Simply download the template you need, edit it to include your specific details, and you're ready to go

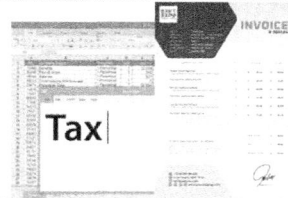

Tax

#5 - Ebook "Advanced Excel Formulas, Pivot and Charts"

You'll learn advanced formula techniques that will allow you to perform complex calculations and data analysis tasks quickly and efficiently

#6 - Ebook "Advanced Skills to Become a Data Analyst"

Unleash your inner analytical genius and learn the advanced skills and techniques necessary to excel in this dynamic field

82% of Jobs Require Proficiency in Excel

Studies Show that You Increase your Chances of Getting Hire by **12%** if You Have Excel Skills

>> SCAN THE FOLLOWING QR CODE TO GO TO EXCEL 2023 BOOK on AMAZON US <<

Chapter 11: Bonus

Thank you so much for reading my book.

I really can't tell you how much it means to me that somebody chose to read something I created.

I hope you enjoyed it as much as I enjoyed writing it.

It took a lot of time, energy, and hard work to write the best possible result for your experience, which is why it would mean a LOT if you could **take just two minutes** from your day and **leave a review on Amazon**. It doesn't have to belong or be detailed - any comment will do.

I know a book may not be enough, so I am offering you the **Video Course 'Excel Fundamental'** and the **Best Ready-to-Use Excel Templates for free**.

Please scan the following QR Code to get the bonuses:

You will receive an email with links to access the various resources. If you do not see my email, please look for it in the spam or another section of your inbox.

If you have any problems, anything from the book you didn't understand, or suggestions to improve the book, feel free to contact me at **nigel@becrepress.com**, and I will respond as soon as possible.

I wish you all the best as you embark on your adventure with Excel, and I hope it opens new doors for you.

Nigel Tillery

Printed in Great Britain
by Amazon